MOVING ON UP
South Asian Women and
Higher Education

MOVING ON UP
South Asian Women and Higher Education

Yasmin Hussain and
Paul Bagguley

Trentham Books

Stoke on Trent, UK and Sterling, USA

Trentham Books Limited
Westview House   22883 Quicksilver Drive
734 London Road   Sterling
Oakhill   VA 20166-2012
Stoke on Trent   USA
Staffordshire
England ST4 5NP

First published 2007

British Library Cataloguing-in-Publication Data
A catalogue record for this book is available from the British Library

ISBN: 978 1 85856 349 7

Designed and typeset by Trentham Print Design Ltd, Chester and printed in Great Britain by Cromwell Press Ltd, Trowbridge.

Contents

Acknowledgements • vi

Introduction • 1

Chapter 1
The Context • 9

Chapter 2
Conceptualising South Asian Women and HE • 27

Chapter 3
Identities: Ethnicity, Britishness and Religion • 37

Chapter 4
Deciding to go to University • 57

Chapter 5
Negotiating University: plans for marriage
and studying at home • 87

Chapter 6
Financial Strategies for Funding a Degree:
the moral economies of family support • 109

Chapter 7
Racism, Islamophobia and Experiences
of University • 121

Chapter 8
Conclusion • 141

References • 145

Subject Index • 153

Acknowledgements

We would like to thank the many people who made this book possible. First and foremost, thanks should go to the many young South Asian women that we interviewed. The research upon which this book is based was made possible by a generous research grant from the Joseph Rowntree Foundation. We were supported over the years by three successive research managers at the Joseph Rowntree Foundation: Mark Hinman, Chris Goulden and Helen Barnard. We also benefited from the support of an advisory group throughout the research, and we would especially like to thank Sabani Banerjee of HEFCE, Dr David Owen, Dr Andrew Pilkington, Dr Yunas Samad, Dr Peter Sanderson, and Dr Laura Turney for their efforts. Aisha Siddiqah and Rahena Mossabir helped with interviewing, and the interviews were transcribed by Jodie Dyson, Marie Ross, Nichola Hutchinson, Angela Jackman, Rukshana Shah, Renata Muncey, Sanam Nazir, Nuzrat Ali and Louise Williams. Jodie Dyson also provided support for the organisation of advisory group meetings. We would also like to thank Helen May and Helene Pierson of the Faculty of Education Social Sciences and Law Research Support Office at the University of Leeds for the financial management of the project. On the publishing side we would like to thank Gillian Klein for her enthusiasm for this project as well as her support and encouragement in bringing it to completion. Of course none of the above are responsible for what follows. Finally, thanks must go to our families whose support has been invaluable throughout our careers and who continue to support us.

For our parents, brothers and sisters

Introduction

This book is concerned with young South Asian women's experiences of higher education. We want to examine why more South Asian women are staying on in education and going to university and what is happening to them as a consequence. These issues are of current considerable policy concern as, whilst many more young South Asian women are staying on in higher education, there are concerns about their concentration in certain institutions (Shiner and Modood, 2002), and mounting evidence that women of Bangladeshi and Pakistani origin in particular remain disadvantaged in the labour market relative to white women even when they have a degree (EOC, 2006; Lindley *et al*, 2006; Peach, 2006). South Asian women are often seen as one of the most excluded and disadvantaged groups in the labour market. They have the lowest levels of labour market participation, and the lowest levels of educational qualifications (Bhopal, 1997a); this situation is changing rapidly (EOC, 2006). In this book we attempt to understand why the participation of South Asian women in higher education, especially from Bangladeshi and Pakistani backgrounds, is rising so fast and what might be learnt from this.

Whilst there have been some previous studies of South Asian women and education, none has previously attempted to compare women of Indian, Pakistani and Bangladesh origin, and consider their situations in the sixth form, during their time at university and after they have graduated. There are still some myths and stereotypes about young South Asian women, especially those who are Muslim, where some professionals in education apparently do not expect them to continue into higher education. This book sets out to understand the wider context of the increasing success of South Asian women in higher education by looking at official statistical sources, as well as drawing upon qualitative interviews with over 100 South Asian women in order to understand their experiences of higher education.

Most of the empirical research reported in this book was concerned with the young women's experiences of education. We talked to young women of Indian, Pakistani and Bangladeshi background in the sixth form, during their time at university and after graduation. We asked about their views and experiences of education; the impact of this on their family lives; their identity, including interaction with parents, siblings and the wider family; peer networks; and the role of characteristics such as gender, age and ethnicity in relation to their experience, aspirations and plans for the future. In addition we have reviewed what has been written before on these issues by other researchers, seeking to provide some details about the community contexts and their diversity that young South Asian women come from.

There are a number of difficult theoretical issues that are raised by the questions addressed in this book, but we have deliberately chosen not to address them in the detail that they perhaps deserve, choosing to highlight instead the subtlety and importance of the empirical findings. There are nevertheless a number of conceptual issues that deserve a mention in passing and that we address in more detail at more pertinent points below.

The first of these concerns the question of how to define ethnicity and identity. We do not consider these issues in terms of the theories of race, except when discussing racism. Our approach is firmly rooted in contemporary debates about new ethnic identities, diaspora and hybridity (Back, 1996; Hall, 1990; Jenkins, 1997; Modood *et al*, 1997; Ranger *et al*, 1996). This is because the young women whose lives are discussed in this book in many ways exemplify the issues addressed in these debates. This new ethnicities paradigm explicitly recognises that racism and power confront ethnic groups, and that ethnic identities are constantly subject to revision and re-thinking in the light of the experience of wider social, cultural and political developments. We have at times used words such as tradition and conservativism often associated with older, more fixed definitions of ethnic identity, but this has been only to paraphrase the accounts of the young women in our interviews.

However, as some readers will no doubt realise, the use of both official statistical sources using official definitions of ethnic groups relies upon a concept of ethnicity that conflicts with that used in qualitative interviews. In the former official definitions, respondents to the Census of Population or those filling in UCAS forms are given a limited choice of ethnic categories with which to identify. This might be termed a categorical definition, one that is imposed on people by the researchers (Jenkins, 1997: 54).

In the latter, during the qualitative interviews the young women themselves defined their own ethnicities. These might be termed as collective self-identifications where the process of ethnic identification is subject to all kinds of influences and nuances (Jenkins, 1997: 55).

Consequently, we have treated the patterns revealed in the analyses of the official statistics as patterns or regularities that are not to be explained by further more complex statistical analysis, but as puzzles to be explained by careful analysis of the qualitative data. By asking the young women about how their thoughts and actions relate to their identities we have aimed to examine how these might plausibly account for the statistical patterns.

The second area of theoretical difficulty concerns the use of terms such as choice and decision. Sociologists are naturally wary of such terms especially in relation to issues around entry to university (Reay *et al*, 2005) as they imply a simple, rational model of decision-making that ignores questions of power and the wider social context. We largely agree with these authors. Readers should be aware that when we use these terms, they are a shorthand for what are quite complex processes of negotiation, often between the young women and their families over long periods of time.

Thirdly, much of the recent research in this field has been strongly influenced by the ideas of cultural capital (Reay *et al*, 2005) and social capital (Crozier and Davies, 2006; Dwyer *et al*, 2006; Modood, 2004). However, we have found these ideas to be of limited use in helping us to understand what is happening in relation to South Asian women and higher education. These approaches tend to produce a list of the characteristics needed to be successful in education, often producing rather essentialised accounts of cultural and social groups. In addition, whilst they are undoubtedly powerful accounts of how class inequality in education is reproduced between generations, we feel that they are of limited use in explaining social change between generations for ethnic groups. Furthermore, in our analysis, the role of the young women in their negotiations with parents and struggles within the education system are difficult to analyse using static ideas like cultural and social capital.

Whilst our overall approach is from within the new ethnicities perspective, we do not feel that this provides all the answers to our empirical puzzles. The rise of the significance of Islamic identities is one case in point, but we have also drawn upon other ideas in order to understand how the young women are managing their finances at university, and their experiences of racism and Islamophobia. In relation to the former, we have found the ideas of strategy and moral economy useful in understanding how the young women managed their finances at university. Their financial management entails strategic thinking in the sense that they had to take account of other people's expectations of them in their decisions about how to finance their university education. In doing this they were often influenced by their own or their families' and communities' moral and religious orientations.

Previous research

Previous research into South Asian women and higher education has either treated them as part of a larger group of ethnic minority students (eg Modood and Shiner, 1994; Connor *et al*, 2004) or focused upon particular groups of South Asian women students, such as Bangladeshis and Pakistanis alone (eg Dale *et al*, 2002), or had relied upon very small samples as part of wider studies of South Asian women and employment (Ahmad *et al*, 2003). Others have focused upon Muslims alone to the neglect of ethnicity and other religious identities amongst British South Asians (Afshar, 1994; Ahmad, 2001). This book is distinctive because it looks at young women of Bangladeshi, Indian and Pakistani backgrounds. Furthermore, they were students or graduates of 'old' universities as well as 'new' universities. Our research was designed to examine groups of young women before, during and after higher education in order to draw out the differences between South Asian women in terms of ethnicity, religion and social class origins.

Young South Asian women are a critically important group to consider for several reasons. First and foremost, women of Bangladeshi and Pakistani origin have the lowest wages of any group of women of any ethnic origin (Leslie and Drinkwater, 1999). Furthermore, 60 per cent of Pakistanis and Bangladeshis are in the lowest fifth of the income distribution, lower than any other ethnic group (Platt, 2002). Secondly, although women of Bangladeshi and Pakistani origin have one of the fastest rates of increase in participation in higher education, they still remain among the most excluded groups from university education.

It is this combination of the country's most severe social and economic exclusion combined with rapid change in an apparently positive direction that makes the issues addressed in this book so important. These issues are given a heightened significance by some of the partial and misleading accounts coming from some political sources (Cantle, 2001; Neville-Jones, 2007) where only the most negative aspects of the position of South Asian women in their communities are selected for comment, and the positive developments or constraints from outside the communities are ignored.

The structure of this book

The following chapter provides an overview of the context of young South Asian women in education and employment. We draw attention to the differences between women of Bangladeshi, Indian and Pakistani origin in terms of income, education, social class and labour market situation. We also emphasise how these circumstances have been changing since the early 1990s. Consequently, a key theme of the chapter and indeed the book as a whole is one of diversity and change. The chapter establishes the diverse circumstances of the different South Asian ethnic groups, as well as raising some questions that we have sought to answer through the qualitative interviews with young South Asian women.

Following this overview of the context of South Asian women and universities, we go on to consider in the next chapter the different analytical, conceptual and theoretical frameworks that have been developed in recent years in order to explain and understand the position of South Asian women in education. We consider the different emphases placed upon class and gender that have emerged from more general studies of inequalities in higher education; questions of ethnicity and racism in education, particularly at university level; the role of religion, especially Islam, in explaining the different levels of participation in higher education found amongst South Asian women; and the role of family and community practices with respect to women and education amongst British South Asians.

Finally in this chapter we consider recent attempts to understand inequalities in higher education and the position of South Asians in particular, using theories of cultural capital and social capital. For those readers interested in such issues, this book develops a critique of currently fashionable approaches to understanding inequality in higher education that draw heavily upon the work of Bourdieu. We have found such approaches extremely limited in making sense of South Asian women's experiences of university.

In chapter 4, we examine the contemporary identities of young South Asian women in the sixth form, at university and after they have graduated. Our approach to identity is grounded in what could be termed the new identities paradigm that has emerged since the 1980s. Central to this approach is to see ethnic identities as processes of individual and collective identity formation in response to wider social, cultural and political developments. It thus challenges notions of ethnic identity that emphasise tradition, continuity and the maintenance of fixed cultural practices. We examine separately how young Bangladeshi, Indian and Pakistani women talk about their ethnic identities.

In addition, we examine how they see themselves in relation to ideas about Britishness and, for Muslims, the significance of religion.

A particularly important expression of ethnic identity for South Asian women is clothing, and the ways in which they dress acts as both a gendered and ethnic public marker of who they are in contemporary universities. At the present time, this makes them the most visible of ethnic minority groups in British universities, consequently this is a further issue to which we give specific attention. This analysis of identity enables us to present in some detail the diverse ethnic and religious positions from which different groups of South Asian women are entering university in Britain today and the potential constraints and distinctive experiences that they face.

Chapter 5 examines how young South Asian women make decisions about going to university. This looks at issues such as which type of university they prefer, their choice of degree subject and whether or not they decide to remain at home whilst at university. We also explore the influences on these decisions, such as the views of parents, siblings and the community. This chapter provides some answers to the issues identified in the discussion of the context such as the concentration of South Asian women in certain subjects at degree level, and the sources of the strong commitment of young South Asian women to higher education.

The following chapter explores in more detail how young South Asian women negotiate their time at university in relation to community and parental expectations about living at home and getting married. This touches upon the issue of arranged marriages and how such practices are evolving with Britain's South Asian communities. As these are often seen as a source of constraint upon women's opportunities for higher education, it is important to examine this issue. We show that there is considerable diversity and flexibility around the issue of marriage and how it is arranged. In terms of the young women's experiences and expectations, whilst arranged marriages are more prevalent amongst the Bangladeshi and Pakistani communities, there is considerable class-related diversity amongst those communities.

A further theme here is the propensity of South Asian women to remain living with their parents whilst studying at university. This practice we found to be more frequent amongst the Muslim women, but there were also other important factors influencing decisions around this issue such as the cost of living away from home. The tendency for many Muslim and working-class South Asian women to stay at home whilst at university often limits their choice of university and degree subject. For them there are geographically circumscribed local markets for higher education.

We have devoted a chapter to the consideration of how young South Asian women are financing their degrees. Although the student finance system for higher education in the UK was re-organised quite soon after we completed our fieldwork, our findings still have an important contemporary relevance. The inequalities generated by the various changes to the student support system since the early 1990s have been the subject of considerable political controversy. Much of the research into this question has been based on quantitative data (Callender, 2003; Callender and Jackson, 2004; Finch *et al*, 2006).

Although this has been essential in order to document the impact of fees and loans, there has been a lack of qualitative data on how students are now managing their finances, and how this might vary between or within particular groups. Bangladeshi and Pakistani Muslims are amongst the most impoverished sections of the community, and they also have religious restrictions on taking out the loans that are now expected to fund higher education. In this chapter we analyse the different moral economies that shape their financial strategies for their time at university.

The following chapter considers young South Asian women's experiences of racism and Islamophobia. Despite appearances to the contrary, universities are not insulated from these phenomena. Whilst much recent work in this area has focused upon institutional racism or the changing content of racist or Islamophobic imagery, consideration of interpersonal experiences of racism and xenophobia has been lacking. Exceptions include some analyses of the experiences of children and other young people, as well as periodic surveys or analyses of official data on reports to the police and prosecutions, but even these fail to specify what is happening within universities.

What we found especially striking was the isolation that some young women experienced at university. These were only overcome on those courses or in those universities where there was a critical mass of other South Asian women students from whom they could seek support. In some instances racist or Islamophobic incidents were so bad that women changed university or considered ceasing to wear the *hijab*. Contrary to widespread belief universities are not havens from racism and xenophobia.

The concluding chapter provides an overview of the main empirical findings of the book as a whole. There we summarise the overall developments in South Asian women's move to university over the past fifteen to twenty years, emphasising the complex processes that lie behind this. We conclude that massive changes in gender relations as well as relationships between generations have taken place and are taking place within Britain's South Asian communities. Consequently many popular political and media images of South Asian women are seriously misleading.

1

The Context

This chapter looks at the patterns and trends in the education and employment of young South Asian women. The past twenty years have been a period of remarkable expansion of higher education in Britain (Archer *et al*, 2003) but the increasing participation of South Asian women, especially those of Bangladeshi and Pakistani origin, has surpassed all expectations. A study completed in the 1980s of Pakistani women Afshar (1989b) concluded that there was little evidence of change in their career and educational aspirations, and suggested that they were rejecting education as a means of upward social mobility. Joly (1995) also foresaw problems if Pakistani parents did not allow their daughters to continue into higher education. Studies of Pakistani communities in particular, often contributed to a rather distorted perception of South Asian women and higher education, in general overlooking the diversity within and between different South Asian communities.

In contrast to these rather pessimistic predictions, research in Lancashire around the same time (Penn and Scattergood, 1992) suggested the opposite scenario for the future, that young Pakistani women were strongly committed to pursuing a university education and had aspirations of going into professional occupations. What then has been the experience since the 1980s of South Asian women's participation in university education? How do the different experiences of Bangladeshi, Indian and Pakistani women compare during this period?

The first studies to examine the inter-relations between gender and ethnicity and university attendance in a systematic way were Vellins (1982) Ballard and Vellins (1985) and Taylor (1993b). This early work on the participation of

South Asians in university education was initially unable to distinguish between those born in the UK and migrants, and those originating from India, Pakistan or Bangladesh (Vellins, 1982). It did, however, reveal the broad preferences of South Asian students for medical and natural sciences and the lower participation of South Asian women compared to men.

Ballard and Vellins (1985) elaborated on these early efforts at measuring the relationship between ethnic origins, gender and university attendance, by distinguishing between Bangladeshi, Indian and Pakistani students, revealing the higher participation rates among Indians compared to Bangladeshis and Pakistanis. On the lower participation rate of Pakistani women, they suggested that religious factors were important in explaining this (Ballard and Vellins, 1985: 262). They also noted the strong propensity of South Asian students to overcome class disadvantages in getting to university, and they emphasised the commitment to education of South Asian parents in spite of the disadvantages built into the education system. These are themes that have recurred in subsequent debates about ethnic origins, gender and access to university.

In table 1.1 opposite we have attempted to produce similar measures of the proportion of young people going to university by ethnic group and gender for the year 2000 to those of Ballard and Vellins (1985). Given the different definitions and data sources over this period of time and other problems with the data, they should be regarded as no more than estimates. Nevertheless they do paint a striking picture of considerable educational advancement by young South Asian people, especially women. There remain significant differences between the university entrance rates of Indian, Pakistani and Bangladeshi people, although the gender differences within each of the South Asian ethnic groups are now modest compared to twenty-five years ago.

National level data on ethnic origin as opposed to country of birth only became available in 1990, following a CRE investigation into racial discrimination in university admissions (Modood, 1993; Taylor, 1993a, 1993b). This showed that South Asian applicants, both men and women, were more likely to be accepted at what were then polytechnics, a trend that has continued since then (Connor *et al*, 2004). This was partly explained by differences in A level results, re-sits and the propensity to choose subjects that require high A level grades. Such institutions are often in locations with high local ethnic minority populations, and Pakistani women in particular were found to prefer local universities (Modood, 1993; Taylor, 1993a, 1993b). It was also suggested that the tendency of Pakistani women to attend a local university was

Table 1.1: Estimated percentages of selected ethnic groups by gender aged 18-19 entering university in 1979 and 2000

1979			2000		
Birthplace	Male	Female	Ethnic Origin	Male	Female
UK	11.0	7.6	White	16.5	17.0
India	12.2	4.2	Indian	26.6	28.5
Pakistan	7.0	1.7	Pakistani	14.7	14.5
Bangladesh	1.8	1.6	Bangladeshi	13.0	12.5

Source: 1979 data Ballard and Vellins, 1985; 2000 data authors' calculations from Census of Population and UCAS data.

due to parental preferences (Singh, 1990). Since the 1980s there has been a continued rapid increase in the numbers of young South Asian women going to University. Table 1.2 below shows the growth of first year full-time undergraduate women studying for degrees for selected ethnic groups. Whilst the percentage increase between 1994-5 and 2004-5 in the numbers of white women commencing undergraduate degrees was 43.3 per cent, that for the South Asian women is much larger. However, there is considerable diversity within the South Asian group. The number of Indian women starting full-time degrees increased by almost twice the rate for white women at 84.8 per cent. The number of Pakistani women starting full-time undergraduate degrees had grown by 158.7 per cent and most dramatically for Bangladeshi women by 273.7 per cent.

This diversity among the South Asian category is a continual theme of this book that we seek to explore and explain in more detail. Of particular concern to us is to understand and explain the rapid growth in university entrance among women of Bangladeshi and Pakistani origin. This growth has to be set within a demographic context where different ethnic groups have different age structures. Table 1.3 below shows the change in size of the 18-24 age group of women, those most likely to be attending university, for selected ethnic groups. It can be seen that, when comparing these two tables, the increase in the numbers going to university has been far greater than the growth in this segment of the population for each ethnic group.

The effect of this increase in university attendance can be seen in the different levels of educational attainment achieved by the younger generations of South Asian women. The following table (1.4) presents an analysis of the

Table 1.2: Percentage change in numbers of first year UK domiciled full-time first degree female students and ethnicity 1994-95 to 2004-05

	White	Indian	Pakistani	Bangladeshi
Percentage increase				
1994-5/2004-05	43.3%	84.8%	158.7%	273.7%
Number in 1994-5	98,125	3,817	1,527	388
Number in 2004-05	140,645	7,055	3,950	1,450

Source: Calculated from HESA table 10b

Table 1.3: All women aged 18-24, England and Wales, 1991-2001 for selected ethnic groups

	1991	2001	Percentage change 1991-2001
White	2,367,544	1,898,094	-19.8%
Indian	50,204	64,905	29.3%
Pakistani	31,278	54,318	73.7%
Bangladeshi	10,322	23,382	126.5%

Source: Census of Population 1991 and 2001

Sample of Anonymised Records (SARS) of the 2001 Census for England and Wales[1]. The percentages of each sex within selected ethnic groups achieving degree level qualifications is shown for age groups from 25-29 to 65 and over. This clearly shows the advances made in higher education by successive age groups of South Asian women. Comparing the 25-29 year olds with the older age groups shows that the proportion of those obtaining degree level qualifications has increased with each successive age group more for South Asian women than for white British women. This is especially so for women of Indian origin. Whilst for all ethnic groups the gender gap between men and women has been narrowed, it still remains substantial among the 25-29 age group for Pakistanis and Bangladeshis. These features again underline the importance of considering the different ethnic groups among South Asians, as well as considering the different experiences of men and women within each ethnic group.

Table 1.4: Percentage with degree level qualifications (level 4/5) by age, sex and selected ethnic groups, England and Wales, 2001

| | Age Groups | | | | |
	25-29	30-44	45-59	60-64	65 and over
British					
Males	29.8%	22.4%	19.1%	14.1%	12.6%
Females	29.7%	21.5%	17.8%	12.7%	11.3%
Indian					
Males	56.8%	39.1%	28.2%	32.0%	31.9%
Females	53.9%	31.4%	21.4%	16.9%	11.6%
Pakistani					
Males	33.2%	27.2%	22.8%	19.4%	12.5%
Females	25.6%	17.4%	13.1%	9.6%	6.7%
Bangladeshi					
Males	24.0%	19.3%	17.8%	19.9%	9.5%
Females	15.5%	10.7%	12.2%	7.7%	4.7%

Source: SARS, Census of Population, 2001

South Asian women at university

It has been known for some time that certain ethnic minority groups are over-represented amongst applicants to university, as students and among graduates, whilst others are under-represented (Connor *et al*, 2004; Modood, 1993; Shiner and Modood, 2002; Taylor, 1993a; 1993b). However, those analyses sometimes did not examine in sufficient detail how far there were significant gender differences within each ethnic group. In some ethnic groups, Bangladeshis for example, young women were much less likely to go to university than young men (Ballard and Vellins, 1985). It is this gendered dimension that we are seeking to examine here in more detail.

In general, Indian and Pakistani young women are more likely to get to university than young white women, whilst young Bangladeshi women are less likely to do so. They have much lower rates of application and entry than the other South Asian ethnic groups. When the gender differences within the ethnic groups are considered, a slightly different picture emerges. White women are more likely than young white men to go to university. The admissions and acceptance rates among young Indian men and women are very similar. However, there are significantly higher rates of application and admission to universities among young Bangladeshi and Pakistani men than

13

among women from those groups. It appears that, in terms of going to university, young Bangladeshi women still experience an ethnic penalty, whilst both young Bangladeshi and Pakistani women experience a gender penalty in comparison to men from these backgrounds (Bagguley and Hussain, 2007).

The following table (1.5) shows the main undergraduate degree subject areas in which South Asian and white female applicants accepted places in 2005. There are five subject areas where South Asian women applicants disproportionately apply to and gain acceptance on degree courses relative to white women applicants: medicine and dentistry; subjects allied to medicine; mathematical and computer sciences; law; business and administrative studies. Together these subject account for around half of the South Asian women's applications and acceptances, compared to about a quarter of the white women's applications and acceptances. Young South Asian women are thus twice as likely as young white women to be aiming for admission to degrees in these subjects. Furthermore, there is very little variation between the different South Asian ethnic groups in this regard, although young Indian and Pakistani women are more likely to be interested in subjects allied to medicine than young Bangladeshi women. This may reflect South Asian parents' preferences for their daughters to aim for traditional professional subjects (Abbas, 2004), an issue that we consider in some detail in the chapters below.

However, we should be wary about this kind of generalisation. Table 2.6 compares the percentage of applicants for the most popular subject groups among South Asians for 1990 and 2005 university entry. This demonstrates that there has been quite a dynamic picture over the past fifteen years. Some of this dynamism undoubtedly arises from the development of new degree programmes that may be attractive to South Asian women applicants, but the broad picture is clear. Over the past fifteen years there has been a noticeable movement of South Asian women applicants away from the subjects that they typically applied for. There has been a shift away from medicine, dentistry, social studies and law towards subjects allied to medicine, business and administrative studies. There is still a concentration in professional, semi-professional and vocationally oriented degrees, but the elite professional degrees of medicine and law are declining in relative popularity amongst South Asian women applying to university.

A further important aspect of the background of those going to university is the type of school that they attended prior to applying to university.

Table 1.5: Pattern of acceptances for female applicants by selected ethnic groups and JASC subject group, 2005 entry

Sum of Female Acceptances	Ethnic Origin			
JACS Subject Group	Bangladeshi	Indian	Pakistani	White
Group A Medicine and Dentistry	2.9%	6.7%	4.3%	2.2%
Group B Subjects allied to Medicine	9.2%	13.9%	15.0%	9.5%
Groups C to F Sciences	9.9%	10.0%	9.1%	14.7%
Group G Mathematical and Computer Sciences	6.4%	4.8%	6.2%	1.8%
Groups H to K Engineering etc	1.8%	2.4%	1.8%	2.0%
Group L Social Studies	11.4%	7.5%	8.5%	8.0%
Group M Law	12.8%	9.6%	13.4%	4.8%
Group N Business and Administrative studies	12.5%	16.8%	14.0%	7.7%
Groups P to Z Humanities etc	33.0%	28.4%	27.6%	49.3%

Source: UCAS, authors' analysis

Table 1.6: Subject distribution of female applicants, 1990-2005

Female Applicants	Ethnic Origin							
JACS Subject Group	Bangladeshi		Indian		Pakistani		White	
	1990	2005	1990	2005	1990	2005	1990	2005
A Medicine and Dentistry	18.9%	7.0%	15.2%	11.4%	17.8%	10.2%	4.2%	3.2%
B Subjects allied to Medicine	5.6%	10.9%	9.5%	14.4%	9.7%	14.7%	3.3%	11.9%
C Biological Sciences	12.2%	8.0%	7.4%	7.7%	9.2%	6.1%	8.1%	12.3%
G Mathematical and Computer Sciences	2.7%	4.2%	4.5%	3.9%	3.7%	4.7%	2.2%	1.4%
H to K Engineering etc	3.7%	1.1%	2.0%	1.5%	2.1%	0.9%	1.9%	1.4%
L/M Social Studies and Law	24.9%	21.5%	23.7%	15.7%	24.0%	19.7%	17.0%	11.6%
N Business and Administrative studies	2.7%	13.0%	10.7%	16.6%	6.9%	14.2%	5.3%	6.9%

Source: 1990 data from Taylor (1993b); 2005 data authors' analysis of UCAS data.

Bangladeshi and Pakistani women starting university in 2005 were more likely to have attended Sixth Form College than those of Indian or white background. In addition, women of Indian or white background were more likely to have attended an independent school than those of Bangladeshi or Pakistani origin (Bagguley and Hussain, 2007). This is important as Reay *et al* (2005) have shown that independent schools give better support to their pupils in general when applying to university. Consequently those women from Bangladeshi and Pakistani backgrounds are likely to be relatively disadvantaged in comparison to white and Indian women for this reason when applying to university.

In terms of A level qualifications for university, there is a distinct pattern of inequality that disadvantages Bangladeshi and Pakistani women when they are applying to university. In 2005, 34.6 per cent of white women accepted at university had 360 or more points (equivalent to three grade As at A level), as did 26.5 per cent of Indian women, but only 18 per cent of Pakistani women and 14.8 per cent of Bangladeshi women (Bagguley and Hussain, 2007) did so. Taylor (1993b) and Modood (1993) found a similar pattern of A level scores amongst applicants in the early 1990s, indicating that this feature of relative educational inequality seems to have changed little in almost a generation. This is significant as Shiner and Modood (2002) suggested that the higher levels of university acceptances among white applicants compared to Bangladeshis and Pakistanis were largely explained by differences in A level scores; we can see how these operate as a significant source of inequality. This is likely to have longer term consequences, as Weale (1993) found that, amongst men at least, higher A level scores of graduates led to higher incomes later in life.

Overall the acceptance rates at university in recent years have been very similar for each ethnic group, although that for Pakistani women is the lowest. Although South Asian women have a lower acceptance rate for medicine and dentistry than white women, for subjects allied to medicine it is rather better for South Asian women, especially those of Indian and Pakistani origin. For maths and computer sciences there is little variation, but some evidence that Bangladeshis accept this as a second best option. Law is an especially competitive subject for entry and, like medicine, the acceptance rates are lower for South Asian applicants, especially Pakistani women (Bagguley and Hussain, 2007).

This fits with evidence from other studies suggesting that South Asian students often re-sit GCSEs and A levels to achieve higher grades (Taylor, 1993a).

Shiner and Modood (2002) suggested that these re-sits were a key reason why ethnic minority students were concentrated in new universities, as established institutions, where there is stronger competition for entry, often did not take re-sits into account. In the analysis of our interviews with the young women, we shall encounter instances where women had to re-sit several times as they were studying subjects that their parents preferred rather than those which they themselves felt were more suitable. A similar process seems to be occurring here: if at first you don't succeed, try try again. For at least some South Asian women, getting to University is what matters in the end, more than the subject studied.

Social class inequalities have been at the forefront of research into inequalities in access to university for some time (Archer *et al*, 2003; Blackburn and Jarman, 1993; Egerton and Halsey, 1993; Halsey *et al*, 1980; Reay *et al*, 2005). However, the systematic examination of how ethnic origin and class origins interact in shaping access to university is more limited. McManus *et al* (1995), Modood (1993) and Shiner and Modood (2002) have noted how class background did not explain ethnic differences in access to university. This excludes the role of different social class origins of different ethnic groups as an explanatory factor, one that is often wheeled out in explaining educational and socio-economic differences.

We explore this question in the following table (2.7) which shows the socio-economic group of the parents of those who accepted degree places in 2005. From this we can see that young white women who get to University are more likely to be from the middle classes than any from the South Asian groups. What is striking about the results for the South Asian groups are the high percentages from routine occupational backgrounds and those for which the occupational background is 'unknown'. A high percentage of young Bangladeshi women also come from semi-routine occupations. The very high percentages for the unknown category may be due to the fact that this information was not provided on the UCAS form, or it may be that the parents of the young women are economically inactive due to unemployment, ill health or retirement. This is partially confirmed by the data we present later on in this chapter on the economic activity and unemployment rates for these groups. In our own interviews we found that a high proportion of the Bangladeshi women reported that their fathers were deceased, retired or unemployed.

Table1.8 below takes this analysis a stage further by looking at the acceptance rates for the different ethnic groups by social class. The data for white female applicants shows a fairly clear gradient from the higher level middle-class

Table 1.7: Female degree acceptances, by selected ethnic groups and socio-economic group of parents, 2005

Socio-Economic Group	Ethnic Origin			
	Bangladeshi	Indian	Pakistani	White
1. Higher managerial and professional occupations	3.2%	12.2%	6.5%	17.9%
2. Lower managerial and professional occupations	9.9%	17.2%	12.6%	26.7%
3. Intermediate occupations	3.4%	10.5%	5.7%	13.1%
4. Small employers and own account workers	9.2%	7.3%	12.7%	5.9%
5. Lower supervisory and technical occupations	0.3%	3.4%	2.3%	4.1%
6. Semi-routine occupations	20.2%	14.4%	11.0%	10.8%
7. Routine occupations	7.2%	7.8%	7.7%	4.4%
8. Unknown	46.7%	27.3%	41.5%	17.1%
Grand Total	100.0%	100.0%	100.0%	100.0%
Total N	1419	7019	4135	150537

Source: UCAS, authors' analysis

socio-economic groups to the lower ones. However, for South Asian female applicants this gradient is not so clear-cut. Indeed the acceptance rates for Pakistani women are higher for those from routine occupational backgrounds than for those from middle-class higher managerial and professional backgrounds.

Generally speaking, for each socio-economic group the acceptance rates for Indian women and white women are higher than those for Pakistani women. This is especially noticeable for those from middle-class higher managerial and professional backgrounds. This suggests that middle-class White women have a class advantage that ethnic minority students do not have. Middle-class Bangladeshi and Pakistani women experience an ethnic penalty when applying to university. They are less likely to be successful in securing a place than their middle-class Indian and white peers. Shiner and Modood (2002) found that when all other factors were taken into account, this was often due to older universities being less likely to offer places to ethnic minority applicants. However, our evidence does not enable us to demonstrate that discrimination is taking place. Overall, the irrelevance of class to understanding

Table 1.8: Acceptance rates of women entering university in 2005 by selected ethnic groups

	Ethnic Origin			
	Bangladeshi	Indian	Pakistani	White
1. Higher managerial and professional occupations	0.79*	0.84	0.73	0.85
2. Lower managerial and professional occupations	0.75	0.83	0.76	0.81
3. Intermediate occupations	0.77	0.81	0.72	0.78
4. Small employers and own account workers	0.82	0.83	0.76	0.78
5. Lower supervisory and technical occupations	0.50*	0.87	0.83*	0.79
6. Semi-routine occupations	0.75	0.82	0.72	0.73
7. Routine occupations	0.80	0.82	0.77	0.74
8. Unknown	0.74	0.78	0.69	0.75
All	0.76	0.81	0.72	0.79

* Numbers of either applicants or acceptances less than 100 in these categories.

Source: UCAS, authors' analysis

South Asian women's access to university seems to have continued since Shiner and Modood's (2002) analysis of university applications in the mid-1990s.

Developments at GCSE and A level

Before people can go on into higher education they need the qualifications to gain entrance to university. Generally speaking, two or more A levels and five or more good GCSEs (grade C or better) are needed. The details of the performance of South Asian pupils at school have been the subject of controversy for some time (Haque, 2000; Tomlinson, 1983). In the early 1980s the apparent high levels of performance of South Asian pupils in public examinations was compared favourably to that of pupils of West Indian origin (Tomlinson, 1983: 381). However, these debates are fraught with problems of over-generalisation about South Asians, and the use of loaded language about 'under-achievement' and 'over-achievement' (Tomlinson, 1983; Troyna, 1984), and some have highlighted how important it is to examine variations within ethnic groups as well as between them (Haque, 2000).

During the 1970s and 80s South Asian pupils were found to be leaving school with fewer qualifications or lower average grades than white pupils. This was especially the case for South Asian girls although the situation was improving over time (Tomlinson, 1983). Subsequent research covering the 1990s (Demack *et al*, 2000) showed that the ethnic inequalities in GCSE performance, measured in terms of passing five GCSEs at grades A to C, had widened between 1988 and 1995. Indian pupils were amongst those who performed the best by 1995, and Bangladeshi and Pakistani pupils were amongst those who experienced the greatest disadvantage. Overall, South Asian girls had higher rates of passing five GCSEs at grades A to C than South Asian boys by 1995. Ethnic inequalities persisted after gender and social class differences were taken into account (Demack *et al*, 2000).

Outcomes at GCSE have changed significantly between 1986 and 1999. For instance, Indian women were performing best at this level by 1999, closely followed by Indian boys. Furthermore, Indian women have improved the most since 1986, followed by Bangladeshi women. In 1999 Bangladeshi women did almost as well as white boys, but less than half of Pakistani women got five or more good GCSEs, and their improvement since 1986 was well behind that of other South Asian women. Only 37 per cent of Pakistani boys and 27.1 per cent of Bangladeshi boys obtained five or more good GCSEs in 1999. Bangladeshi boys had improved the least since 1986 (Bagguley and Hussain, 2007). Obtaining five or more good GCSEs is generally seen as a prerequisite for entering the sixth form in order to study A levels. Generally speaking, regardless of ethnic origin, women are improving at this level more than men, a finding recently confirmed by the Equal Opportunities Commission (EOC, 2006).

In terms of outcomes at A level, there is a broadly similar pattern of results with Indian women and boys both having the largest percentages for passing two or more A levels and obtaining the highest average grades. Only one third of Pakistani and Bangladeshi women have two or more A levels, whilst only one quarter of Pakistani and Bangladeshi boys have these qualifications (Bagguley and Hussain, 2007). In conclusion, Bangladeshi and Pakistani women would appear to be still at a significant disadvantage compared to women from White and Indian backgrounds. This is a key factor that others have suggested largely explains both the lower rates of application and admission to university and the concentration of South Asian students in new universities (Shiner and Modood, 2002).

South Asian women, higher education and the labour market

The position of South Asian women in the labour market has been the focus of a considerable amount of research (Ahmed *et al*, 2003; Brah, 1993; Dale *et al*, 2002; Lindley *et al*, 2006; West and Pilgrim, 1995). These studies have shown that South Asian women are much less likely to be economically active than white women. Among those aged 16 to 24, white women are more likely to be in employment or looking for work. However, within the South Asian group, Indian women are more likely to be economically active at this age than Pakistani or Bangladeshi women. Among those aged 25 and over, this pattern is rather different with Indian and white women having almost identical economic activity rates. In comparison, only a quarter of Pakistani women in this age group are working or looking for work, and only 18 per cent of Bangladeshi women are doing so (Bagguley and Hussain, 2007; Dale *et al* 2002; 2006; EOC, 2006). Consequently, much of what was previously thought to be a lower level of labour market participation by South Asian women in general, is in fact largely found amongst women from Bangladeshi and Pakistani backgrounds.

Furthermore, data from the 2001 Census show that Pakistani women and Bangladeshi women aged 16 to 24 are much more likely to be unemployed among those who are economically active. In contrast, white women and Indian women are more likely to be in full-time employment than Bangladeshi or Pakistani women. In addition, a third of the economically inactive Pakistani and Bangladeshi women in this age group are looking after the home, whilst economically inactive White women and Indian women are much more likely to be students. Among those aged 25 and over, Pakistani and Bangladeshi women are also more likely to be unemployed if they are economically active, and more likely to be looking after the home if they are economically inactive (Bagguley and Hussain, 2007). People of Bangladeshi or Pakistani origin are amongst the poorest in the country (Department of Work and Pensions, 2006), and women of Pakistani or Bangladeshi origin are among the lowest paid in the workforce (Low Pay Commission, 2005).

There is considerable debate about the reasons for these patterns, but it is likely that for older women a combination of lack of suitable qualifications, language skills for the first generation migrants, marriage and childcare responsibilities and lack of opportunities in their local labour markets all play a role (Brah, 1993).

One of the key questions to arise from these findings is to what extent does higher education affect economic activity and unemployment? Table 1.9

enables us to address this issue by drawing upon data provided in a study using the 2001 Census of Population by Clark and Drinkwater (2005). Level 4/5 qualifications are the result of higher education and generally we can see that people with these qualifications have lower levels of unemployment. However, unemployment rates for Indian women graduates are twice those for white women, and unemployment rates for Pakistani and Bangladeshi women graduates are about four times higher. There are two important points here. Whilst being a graduate massively reduces the risk of unemployment for all women in these ethnic groups, Pakistani and Bangladeshi women still experience a significant ethnic penalty. A more detailed analysis of other data by Lindley *et al* (2006) has suggested that discrimination in the labour market was the only factor that was likely to explain this.

Table 1.9: Unemployment rates by selected ethnic groups and highest qualification: England and Wales 2001

Percentages	Male		Female	
	No quals	Level 4/5	No quals	Level 4/5
White	9.8	3.1	6.7	2.4
Indian	11.5	4.0	9.0	5.7
Pakistani	19.3	9.6	25.3	10.9
Bangladeshi	23.1	11.6	40.6	8.2

Source: Clark and Drinkwater, 2005: tables 3 and 4

A further important aspect of employment concerns the levels of the jobs that are held by South Asian women. Pakistani and especially Bangladeshi women are under-represented in management jobs compared to white and Indian women, but they tend to be over-represented in sales occupations (Bagguley and Hussain, 2007). However, what is the picture for the women with degree level qualifications from these groups? Women with first degrees or their equivalent are concentrated in the highest level jobs in terms of social class as shown in table 1.10 below. Over 75 per cent of highly educated women with a white British background are in professional or managerial occupations. However, only 65 per cent of Indian women, and 60 per cent of Pakistani and Bangladeshi women are in these types of position. Highly educated South Asian women are much more likely to be in skilled non-manual jobs than white British women. This demonstrates the considerable labour market advantages that may accrue to those with a university education, however, South Asian women are less likely than their white counterparts to obtain these advantages. This finding is more widely confirmed in recent research by the Equal Opportunities Commission, where employer discrimination against Bangladeshi and Pakistani women has been suggested as a major factor explaining the disadvantages that they experience (EOC, 2006).

Table 1.10 Social class position of women from selected ethnic groups with level 4/5 education, England, Wales and Northern Ireland 2001

Percentages	Ethnic Groups			
	White British	Indian	Pakistani	Bangladeshi
I Professional, Etc.	10.1	19.6	16.5	16.0
II Managerial And Technical	65.8	44.5	43.9	44.2
III N Skilled -Non-Manual	15.3	26.0	26.8	26.5
III M Skilled -Manual	4.6	4.5	3.3	5.5
IV Partly Skilled	3.9	4.9	9.0	7.2
V Unskilled	0.4	0.4	0.5	0.6
Total	100.0	100.0	100.0	100.0
Total N	78971	2748	665	181

Source: SARS (NB: some of the cell percentages are based on very small numbers for Pakistani and Bangladeshi women in the lower social classes)

It is against this national background of the increasing participation of South Asian women in higher education that our qualitative research in West Yorkshire and the West Midlands has been carried out. In pursing that qualitative work we were concerned to try as far as practically possible to represent the diversity amongst South Asian women in terms of ethnic origins, religion, class and educational backgrounds.

Methodology of the present study

Two research sites, Birmingham and Leeds, were chosen after an examination of data from the 2001 Census of Population and a consideration of the types of university located in the cities. Both Leeds and Birmingham have Russell Group universities as well as large new universities. Previous studies of South Asian women and higher education had taken place in Greater Manchester (Dale *et al*, 2002), and London (Ahmad *et al*, 2003), and more general studies of inequalities in higher education had also been based in the greater London area (Archer *et al*, 2003; Reay *et al*, 2005). Leeds was the principal research location where a majority of the interviews took place, and the research in Birmingham involved interviewing fewer people but with the same questions in order to validate the findings from Leeds.

We found no noticeable differences in the data between the two cities, and we have reported the results in terms of the main issues and factors rather than separately for the two cities. Our aim was to interview young South Asian women from Bangladeshi, Indian and Pakistani backgrounds as previous research had focused on only one of these groups or conflated the differences between them. Furthermore we aimed to interview sixth-formers, current undergraduates and recent graduates to get a picture of the whole process of deciding to go to university through to graduating.

Table 1.11 below provides details of the overall sizes of the main South Asian ethnic groups compared to whites in Leeds and Birmingham from the Census of Population for 1991 and 2001. Each of the South Asian groups constitutes a larger percentage of the population in Birmingham than in Leeds.

Table 1.11: Selected ethnic groups in Leeds and Birmingham, 1991 and 2001

Ethnic Groups: 1991-2001				
	1991	2001	1991	2001
	Leeds	Leeds	Birmingham	Birmingham
All people (number)	680722	715402	961041	977087
White	94.2	91.9	78.5	70.4
Indian	1.5	1.7	5.3	5.7
Pakistani	1.4	2.1	6.9	10.7
Bangladeshi	0.3	0.4	1.3	2.1
Other ethnic groups	2.8	5.2	8	11.2

Source: Census of Population 1991 and 2001, ONS

We spoke to 114 young women in all, of whom 37 were Indian, 51 Pakistani and 26 Bangladeshi. Around a third of them were still in the sixth form (39), a third were at university (43) and, as we wanted to know what happened after their graduation, a third were recent graduates (32). The interviews were anonymised; those interviewed were asked to choose their own pseudonyms and we have used these when quoting from interviews. Interviewees were approached in a variety of ways. Undergraduates and current sixth-formers were largely approached in the public social areas of their institutions. Some current postgraduates were also contacted in this way. In addition, some students and many of the recent graduates were contacted through local community centres. The samples were further boosted through snowball sampling.

This sampling strategy enables us to compare the experiences of women from different South Asian ethnic groups at different stages of their educational careers. Furthermore, the size and diversity of the samples means that we can make meaningful comparisons between Indian women of different religious backgrounds. For each of the ethnic groups we are also able to draw out the differences according to the educational levels and social class backgrounds of their parents. Consequently this relatively large sample for a qualitative study means that we can overcome some of the difficulties arising from a focus on a particular ethnic group and other biases that have affected previous studies in this area.

The interviews typically lasted between 45 minutes and one and a half hours and were characterised by a relatively informal style whilst retaining a thematic, topic-centred approach. Although we did not have a rigidly structured list of questions, the interviews explored a number of interrelated themes including the following: personal views and experiences of education, the impact of the young women's education on their family lives, including interaction with parents, siblings and the wider family; their definitions of their identity; peer networks; the role of characteristics such as gender, age and ethnicity in relation to their experiences in education and their aspirations and plans for the future.

Consequently, the interviews were of a semi-structured format to ensure that the specific themes of the research project were addressed, whilst facilitating the option of pursuing particular lines of investigation unique to the individual circumstances of each interviewee. They were conducted at times and places of each young woman's choosing. The interviews were tape-recorded (with the respondents' agreement), translated where appropriate, and fully transcribed.

In the analysis we have reconstructed the key themes from these texts through a thematic analysis of the young women's views and experiences. In particular, when these have emerged as relevant, similarities and differences of ethnic origins, class backgrounds, age and religion have been highlighted and discussed in more detail.

In the next chapter we discuss the various approaches that have been taken by previous writers in the study of South Asian women's position in higher education. We consider both quantitative and qualitative studies, and we are at pains to emphasise how some of those studies are limited by their timing or highly specific samples of respondents. Finally, we are also critical of the recent tendency to oversimplify questions of ethnic identity and to place too much emphasis on the concepts of cultural and social capital in explaining South Asian educational success in contemporary Britain.

Note

1 The Sample of Anonymised Records is a detailed 3% sample of individuals from the 2001 Census of Population. It enables users to construct their own customised tables that are not normally provided by the main Census publications. This work is based on SARS provided through the Centre for Census and Survey Research of the University of Manchester with the support of ESRC and JISC. All census data are Crown Copyright Reserved.

2

Conceptualising South Asian Women and Higher Education

Recent years have seen an upsurge in academic research into finances of university students, their experiences of university, inequalities between them and how they choose which university to attend (Archer *et al*, 2003; Callender, 2003; Connor *et al*, 2001; Forsyth and Furlong, 2000; Reay *et al*, 2005). This has been driven by the increasing numbers attending university, changes to how students finance their university education as well as the broader realisation that universities play a critically important role in the reproduction of wider social inequalities.

Whilst much of this work has been particularly concerned with class inequalities amongst university students, some research since the early 1980s has considered ethnic inequalities in access to higher education (Ballard and Vellins, 1984; Connor *et al*, 2004; Law *et al*, 2004; McManus *et al*, 1995; Modood, 1993; Taylor, 1993a; Vellins, 1982). The most striking findings from this earlier wave of research were those which demonstrated that by the early 1990s many young people from ethnic minority groups were more likely to get to university than white people.

One group that attracted quite a lot of interest at this stage was that of South Asian women. This was because increasing numbers of them were going to university, and this challenged dominant academic and popular perceptions of young South Asian women as docile, uninterested in education and destined via arranged marriages to futures in the private domestic sphere of the family. This group would thus constitute what Yin (1984) called a unique or extreme case – they confounded established expectations about them. Subsequently there were a number of small-scale qualitative studies of South Asian women and their experiences of university (Ahmad, 2001; Ahmed *et al*, 2003; Bhopal, 1998; Dale *et al*, 2002; Housee, 2004).

From this literature a number of analytical themes have emerged, and in this chapter we critically review these in order to establish our own perspective. Broadly speaking, these analytical themes are as follows: issues of class and gender that have emerged from more general studies of inequalities in higher education; questions of ethnicity and racism in education and in universities in particular; the role of religion, especially Islam in explaining the different levels of participation in higher education found amongst South Asian women; family and community practices with respect to women and education amongst British South Asians. Cutting across these analytical themes are the broader concepts of cultural capital and social capital, developed from the work of Bourdieu (1997) and Coleman (1997) which seem to dominate current explanations of higher educational differences with respect to both class (Reay *et al*, 2005) and ethnicity (Modood, 2004).

Ethnicity, racism and access to university

Both Modood and Shiner (1994) and Jones (1993) were among the first to find significant differences in participation in higher education between ethnic groups, in relation to both institutions and subjects. Africans, African-Asians, Chinese, Indian and the other groups were all found to have higher percentages with degrees than the white group in subsequent analyses of the 1991 Census (Owen *et al*, 1997). The issue of racism was also found to be important in this context. In the studies by Modood and Shiner (1994) and Shiner and Modood (2002), UCAS datasets were used to identify whether there is a systematic bias against candidates from ethnic minority groups in the allocation of higher education places. Multivariate analysis suggested that the ethnic differences in the rates of success cannot be fully explained by A Level grades (actual or predicted), the number of A Levels taken, the number of sittings attended, patterns of application, or socio-demographic profile, but left open the possibility that some of the differences are due to discrimination. Evidence of racial discrimination was also uncovered in relation to admissions to medical schools. South Asian students in particular were seen to be disadvantaged due to racial discrimination using their surnames as ethnic markers (McManus *et al*, 1995, 1998).

Compared with the white majority, a higher proportion of South Asians continue in full-time education with a rate of enrolment on degree courses double that of the white norm. Yet they still continue to suffer the same forms of discrimination and exclusion as their parents (Ballard, 1994). Children of parents with higher education were normally likely to pursue higher qualifications themselves (Modood *et al*, 1997). However, Anwar (1998) found that great emphasis was placed on education by South Asian parents irrespective of whether they had higher levels of education themselves: 'education is valued highly within the community as a primary means of improving life chances and is regarded as a self-defining and personally empowering process' (Anwar, 1998: 35). High rates of unemployment for South Asians, especially those without qualifications, and the knowledge that ethnic minorities suffer much higher rates of unemployment, are reasons often cited for the high stay-on rates in higher education. Furthermore the motivation behind this was thought to have come from the ethic of self- improvement that the first generation migrants have for themselves and for their children (Modood *et al*, 1997). This may be no more than the familiar pattern of children performing on average similarly to their parents, with social mobility through education being a gradual process (Halsey *et al*, 1980). What these early quantitative studies thus established was that there was considerable diversity amongst ethnic minority groups and that, although some had higher levels of entry into higher education than the white community, racism was still an important issue in this area.

Studies of South Asian women and education

Many have attempted to examine the relationship between ethnicity, gender and educational achievement amongst South Asian women (eg Abbas, 2004; Wilson, 1978; Westwood and Hoffman, 1979; Tanna, 1990; Wade and Souter, 1992; Penn and Scattergood, 1992; Ghuman, 1994). However, the bulk of these studies have focused upon school attainment, often assuming in some of the earliest studies that South Asian women do not go to university.

Examining the relationship between gender, ethnicity and higher education enables us to explore the issue of difference for South Asian women. The existence and nature of ethnic and gender differences in attainment in national qualifications are significant factors in determining future educational and employment prospects, and are of particular relevance to the consideration of equality in access to such opportunities.

Personal and anecdotal evidence was provided by Seth (1985: 70), who argued that the need for education by South Asian families is frequently an economic one, with mothers: 'most anxious about their children's, especially daughters', educational achievement'. The barrier preventing wider participation in higher education, according to Seth (1985), was that South Asian women receive little support from careers officers, with these cautious attitudes reflecting unfounded stereotyped images of their home background holding them back from higher education.

Shaw's (1994) research on the Pakistani community in Oxford, demonstrated that, whilst only a small minority of girls at that time had gained higher qualifications, they had stayed within the community, finding few problems in combining career with an arranged marriage and participation in family and community events. In contrast to this, the research of Bhopal (1997b, 2000) examined the intersection of gender and ethnicity with specific reference to South Asian women in Britain, in terms of how education and religion impact upon women's responses to the issue of dowries. It found an inverse relationship between educational levels and the acceptance of arranged marriages and the practice of dowries.

The study made by Dale *et al* (2002) of education and labour market prospects for Pakistani and Bangladeshi women found higher levels of labour market participation for Pakistani and Bangladeshi women who had higher level qualifications. The contrast between Shaw's (1994) findings that only a few Pakistani women went on to university compared to these recent findings highlights the scale of change within these communities (Ahmad, 2001; Abbas, 2004). Kalra's (1980) account of young Sikh women fulfilling their parents' expectations and staying at home after leaving school also contrasts with today's situation. Some of these early studies are now seriously out of date due to social change within South Asian communities, and provide a misleading picture of the current experiences of South Asian women in education.

Consequently, knowledge is still relatively limited about how education is viewed among young South Asian women, and especially how far it has changed and the sources of diversity. It is therefore important to focus on the way in which these individuals are disadvantaged in terms of educational opportunities – is it simply domestic or community constraints or are there external institutional factors at work? Currently existing research findings do not address these key questions adequately.

Choices over the uptake of post-compulsory education for South Asian women are much more complex than for their male counterparts or their white female counterparts. Asian women's educational and employment choices may be influenced not just by structural and human capital factors, but also by cultural expectations and family and community pressures. Therefore an understanding of the perceptions of community values and the general context in which these young women make decisions about marriage, family formation and employment are relevant and important (Ahmad, 2001; Dale *et al*, 2002).

Family and community practices and education

Amongst the older generation of women there is often an acceptance of their role within the home to the extent that questions about education and paid employment seemed inappropriate and irrelevant. Literature concerning young South Asian women suggests that their experiences are the product of ideologies, social practices and social structures where racism and class are key determinants. Consequently these women are presented in the popular imagination, and some academic texts, as meek, mild and docile, burdened by family pressures with no hope of pursuing their ambitions and desires (Afshar, 1994; Kalra, 1980; Khanum, 1995). Obstacles hindering progression are highlighted in this literature not as external factors such as the education system but within the home and their community. Having greater domestic responsibilities and less freedom to pursue leisure activities are further deemed indicative of these women's experiences. Some of these studies often conflate the religious values of Islam with cultural expectations.

To a large extent, factors such as religion, country of birth and the presence of children in the household are particularly relevant for South Asian women's decisions about education and employment (Dale *et al*, 2006). The family is an important institution within the South Asian community and very influential on decisions made by its members (Dale *et al*, 2002).

But to what extent do families encourage young women to pursue higher education or is this due to the individuals themselves? According to Ahmad *et al* (2003), the support of the family is important and significant for young women who want to pursue higher education or a career. Parents are keen to see their children do well and not to miss out on the opportunities they didn't have. In these studies all parents wanted their children to do well and encouraged them in their education (Anwar, 1998; Bhatti, 1999).

Some studies have suggested that there was a gender differentiation in parental support (Bhatti, 1999), with the mothers being keener to see their daughters succeed academically and professionally. Many older women without formal qualifications themselves were keen for their daughters to succeed academically and professionally (Bhatti, 1999). In contrast to these findings, more recent research has identified the positive role played by fathers – a finding which challenges stereotypes of 'restrictive' South Asian fathers (Ahmad, 2003). Previous research suggests that parents are supportive of their daughters' pursuit of their educational goals as well as their integration within the employment market.

Questions also need to be raised about the reasons for pursuing higher education from the perspective of the young women in comparison to their parents. How far and in what ways do the views of parents and their daughters differ? For some women and their families in some studies, a positive consequence of higher education and economic activity was improved marriage prospects (Ahmad *et al*, 2003). This research also found that younger women in professional employment are taking alternative approaches to marriage which result in a re-negotiation rather than a rejection of arranged marriages.

For much of the Bangladeshi and Pakistani community in Britain it is important that girls should avoid any behaviour that might damage the family honour (*izzat*) (Bhopal 1997a; 1997b; 2000; Joly, 1995; Kalra, 1980; Shaw, 2000). According to some, South Asian women who live away from home complicate this, as un-chaperoned women provide 'fertile ground for malicious gossip' (Brah, 1993: 143). Such gossip damages family honour. The family would suffer in the community and the young woman would no longer be seen as an acceptable marriage partner (Afshar, 1994). The continuation of post-16 education for girls places them in situations where parents are not able to police the activities of their daughters.

There are considerable variations in the way that the notion of *izzat* impinges on young women. Some researchers have reported that, for the traditional families, curbing the activities of their daughters is important to the extent of chaperoning them to FE Colleges and university. Yet other families allowed their daughters to move away from home and trusted them to behave in an appropriate way. Young women often engaged in a process of negotiation with parents that, at least for some, resulted in being allowed to continue in education. Continuing in further education within their area of residence posed less of a threat than travelling to an institution outside of the local area, according to Dale *et al* (2002). However, most of these studies have focused upon working-class Pakistani communities, especially those originating from Mirpur and, to a lesser extent, Bangladeshis and Sikhs. Consequently, it is difficult to generalise from them and to consider the variations within and between communities arising from educational and social class backgrounds.

Previous research has thus demonstrated the significance of both ethnic difference and gender in relation to higher education and employment for

South Asian women. Furthermore it has identified a series of potential factors within the institutions of higher education and within the ethnic minority communities that contribute to the various patterns and outcomes that they have identified. A particular bias in much of this literature is to focus upon Pakistani communities, especially from Mirpur, which some see as more conservative on these issues and, to a lesser extent, Bangladeshi and Sikh communities.

A question of capitals: class, ethnicity and gender

The concepts of cultural capital (Bourdieu, 1997) and social capital (Coleman, 1997) have come to dominate contemporary interpretations of inequalities in higher education as much as other parts of the sociology of education. The cultural capital school (eg Reay *et al*, 2005) have focused more upon class inequalities and tend to treat ethnic inequalities in higher education as closely related to class, whilst the social capital school (eg Modood, 2004) has seen ethnicity in itself as a distinct causal factor independent of class when explaining ethnic differences in access to university. However, there are several weaknesses in both of these approaches from our perspective.

Firstly, many discussions of the role of social capital in relation to South Asians and education (eg Crozier and Davies, 2006; Dwyer *et al*, 2006; Modood, 2004) elide the distinction between social capital and cultural capital. If social capital is primarily about networks and trust, and cultural capital about values and norms, then it is clear that some discussions which emphasise social capital as 'community or shared values' (Dwyer *et al*, 2006: 10) are blurring a crucial conceptual distinction.

In their work it is clear that it is norms and values (or cultural capital) that are doing the explanatory work, rather than the extent, density and quality of social networks, relationships of trust or social capital. This probably arises from their reliance upon Coleman's definition of social capital which includes norms as a form of social capital alongside social networks, and its subsequent development by others (Coleman, 1997). It is important to maintain this analytical distinction in our view, as cultural capital may favour education, but social capital might be weak and vice versa. In the case of South Asian women going to university, we would suggest that social capital is strong, and that it is cultural capital that has changed.

Secondly, like all capital theory, explanations based on cultural and social capital are very strong on explaining the reproduction of educational inequalities, but relatively weak in explaining change in educational performance. For our purposes this is a serious limitation. From the perspectives of both social capital and cultural capital types of explanation, one would not expect any significant change in educational achievement for ethnic minority groups. At this point it is often noted that it is the second generation of migrants who are educationally successful, and they are benefiting from the social capital of their migrant parents (Crozier and Davies, 2006). However, this elides a crucial empirical point. The second generation have not always been educationally successful. Our problem is how to explain change not just between generations, but within communities. It is clear from our evidence below that this is precisely what has been happening in, for instance, some Bangladeshi and Pakistani communities.

Thirdly, these are profoundly gendered phenomena. Whilst the social capital theorists often note this, they often fail to engage fully with its implications. Social capital itself can be a gendered phenomenon and, in terms of education for South Asian women, female contacts and role models within ethnic groups are extremely important. Ethnic social capital alone is insufficient. Furthermore, the recent rapid growth in the numbers of Bangladeshi and Pakistani women going to university implies not just a transformation of their positioning in terms of their ethnicity, but also in terms of gender relations and practices within their communities.

This is a question not just of social capital, of social networks changing, but rather of cultural norms and expectations being transformed. If one were to remain within Bourdieu's framework, it would appear that new cultural capital has been formed that is now enabling Bangladeshi and Pakistani women to gain access to higher education. However, the problem remains of how to explain this development.

Fourthly, there is no adequate explanation of the origins of social capital. Where does it come from? It is assumed to emerge with the process of settlement of ethnic minority migrant groups, and amongst families (Crozier and Davies, 2006). What social capital theory lacks is an account of the primitive accumulation of social capital in the first place. What is critical here is the ability of a community to build upon individual experiences of higher education in a positive way. It should be recalled that, until relatively recently, many studies reported that parents in the Sikh, Pakistani and Bangladeshi communities were quite strongly opposed to their daughters staying in education beyond the age of 16 (Joly, 1995; Kalra, 1980; Wade and Souter, 1992). This situation has now changed quite dramatically as our findings below demonstrate, and both social capital theory and cultural capital explanations are of little help in understanding this.

In summary, the limited use of the idea of social capital as social networks, especially in our case operationalised in terms of family and friends as sources of advice, support and role models, can be quite productive. However, there are other challenges where it is lacking, especially if one is interested in understanding rapid social change.

Similarly, the closely related idea of cultural capital and the associated concept of habitus face problems when scrutinised closely. Firstly, they tend to essentialise the notion of culture. In many accounts it is often assumed that a social group, typically a social class, shares a series of cultural characteristics, tastes or dispositions. Alternatively these may be expressed as the norm or average around which a social group tends to cluster. However, empirical evidence suggests that classes do not possess such strong cultural dispositions (Barone, 2006). When applied to an ethnic group this approach would tend to represent them as sharing an unchanging set of traditional perspectives or cultural frameworks. However, these kinds of assumption about the cultural homogeneity of ethnic origin have also been challenged (Hall, 1990). What is lost here is all sense of the dynamism of culture, and of the creativity of people's agency with respect to cultural practices and identity.

Secondly, for our purposes the use of the concept of cultural capital often fails to specify the precise mechanisms, processes or practices by which it achieves its effects. The arguments that draw upon cultural capital theory often thus appear to be tautologous. Precisely how particular cultural perspectives or a particular habitus are translated into educational success often remains obscure or unstated (Nash, 1999). This seems to us to be especially the case when applied to ethnic minority groups.

Finally, whilst cultural capital theory can be very effective at achieving what it was originally designed for, namely explaining the reproduction of educational inequalities, it is especially weak at helping with the central task of this book which is explaining the transformation of educational inequalities. There is no space within the theory for explaining how circumstances may change. As Mouzelis (1995) has argued, Bourdieu's theory outlines the social positions that people occupy and their cultural correlates, but fails to consider how interaction might actually unfold. As we shall see in the remainder of this book, this is a critical issue to consider if we are to understand adequately the changing position of South Asian women in British higher education today.

In contrast to these attempts to produce overarching theoretical frameworks, we have taken a middle-range approach (Merton, 1963) where particular concepts and explanations are recognised to have a specific relevance and limited scope. For example, where we identify a range of different types of moral economy that shape different categories of students' strategies for financing their education, or where the concept of critical mass is introduced to help us make sense of students' differing experiences of racism on different courses and at different universities. Most important from our perspective is to understand the changing ethnic identities of South Asian women and their communities in contemporary Britain, and that is the task that we set out to address in the next chapter.

3

Identities: Ethnicity, Britishness and Religion

Since the early 1990s, debates around the concept of identity have become central to understanding the position of ethnic minority groups in Britain (Back, 1996; Hall, 1990; Jenkins, 1997; Modood *et al*, 1997; Ranger *et al*, 1996; Rutherford, 1990). Whilst earlier conceptualisations of ethnicity and identity were criticised for producing stereotyped accounts of ethnic minority groups (Parmar, 1982), the 'new ethnicities' (Hall, 1990) paradigm has been explicitly founded on the recognition of both the agency of ethnic groups to redefine their identities, and to explore the diversity within them in terms of gender, class, religion, etc. 'Consequently, ethnic identities are conceptualised in a more fluid manner, as being constantly re-negotiated, re-defined and re-framed in response to social, cultural and political developments' (Hall, 1990). Whilst much of this work has been associated with attempts to understand the cultural representations produced by different ethnic minority groups (Hall, 1990; Hussain, 2005), it has proved equally useful in understanding the everyday lives of people from different ethnic groups (Back, 1996; Dwyer, 1999a). These have often demonstrated how identity is contextual, multiple and mutable at the level of everyday life involving negotiations between ethnic identities, religious identities and Britishness (Dwyer, 1999a; Hussain and Bagguley, 2005; Rassool, 1999).

Central to this new wave of thinking about ethnicity and identity have been the concepts of diaspora and hybridity (Hall, 1990; Hussain, 2005; Kalra *et al*, 2005). Whilst the concept of diaspora has been deployed with a variety of meanings (Hussain, 2005; Kalra *et al*, 2005; Vertovec, 1996), here we make use of only some of these specific meanings.

In particular, the concept is useful for us when it refers to a sense of ethnic identity as rooted in a place of geographical origin from which a community has migrated, continues to migrate and with which the community may retain trans-national contacts. These understandings of diaspora as an on-going process of trans-national community formation evoking collective memories challenge ideas of a fixed essential home (Brah, 1993; Hussain, 2005). This idea of diaspora entails considerations of the processes of migration and the desire to maintain a sense of collective cultural identity after migration, as well as the role of nation formation in South Asia in the context of political struggles again British colonialism in the last century, and in the case of Bangladesh against Pakistan. Some of these struggles continue to shape the formation of ethnic identities in Britain as in the case of Kashmir for some Pakistanis and Khalistan for some Sikhs (Hussain and Bagguley, 2005; Drury, 1996). For the young women in this study, this often expresses itself in the ways in which they talk about themselves as British-Bangladeshi, British-Pakistani or British-Indian.

This brings us to the question of hybridity and hyphenated identities. The value of this way of approaching ethnic identity is that it highlights how ethnic minority identities, particularly for the young women who are second-generation migrants considered in this book, are constructed across difference (Papastergiadis, 1997). As we shall see, the young women talk about themselves as being British and South Asian and having a religious identity. This does not involve some irreconcilable conflict for them, but rather they have become cultural navigators (Ballard, 1994) negotiating their practices across the differences between their parents' culture, their religion and British culture. Here is underscored again the ways in which ethnic identity is not fixed and immutable, but an ongoing achievement, a political and cultural process.

For younger Muslims in particular, religion has become a source of collective identity as significant as or more significant than any other (Jacobson, 1997; Samad, 1996). There are two perspectives on why this is so. The first emphasises the distinctiveness of religious as opposed to ethnic identity. In this view religion, in this case Islam, is universally applicable, whilst ethnic identities are particularistic and associated with tradition or culture. Furthermore, ethnicity carries connotations of a sense of origin, whereas Islam brings a sense of belonging to a global community – the *umma*. Islam provides detailed rules for everyday life, in contrast to the traditions of caste, dowries, dress, arranged marriages, etc. which are seen as features of a pre-Islamic South Asian culture (Jacobson, 1997). The risk in this perspective is to see ethnicity as an unchanging tradition-bound way of life. However, it does show how people often draw the distinction for themselves between Islam and their ethnic identity.

The second perspective sees the development of the assertion of an Islamic identity as the outcome of a complex political process operating locally, for example the *Satanic Verses* affair, and globally, for example the first Gulf War. The response of the wider society was to demonise all Muslims, thus ignoring the complex set of different identities of the first-generation migrants, en-compassing caste, doctrinal divisions within Islam as well as *biradri* networks (Samad, 1996). In this case, the risk is that we have an over-politicised account. As we shall see below, aspects of both approaches can help us to understand the identities of our respondents.

Linked to these more general developments have been more specific debates about the uses of the terms of 'black' 'Asian', etc. where it has been argued that the generic term 'Black' obscures important social, cultural and political differences (Modood, 1993). A further concern here has been how to consider the rise of the significance of religious, and especially Muslim, identities among younger South Asian people in relation to wider political develop-ments (Hussain and Bagguley, 2005; Samad, 1996). Considering identity in terms of 'Black' or 'ethnic minority' alone is inadequate except in the most general terms.

Despite these developments, thinking about ethnic minority identities in relationship to higher education seems to have overlooked their significance. Consequently there are important recent studies of ethnic minorities and higher education that have retained the use of the term 'black' for example to describe all ethnic minority students (Bird, 1996). Alternatively, there have been attempts to talk rather simplistically of 'ethnic choosing' (Ball *et al*, 2002) in relation to decisions about which university people attend. These studies tend to overlook significant differences among ethnic minority students in their experiences of higher education due not only to ethnic diversity but, as we show later, to gender and religion as well. This is in striking contrast to many other studies that have recognised the diversity of experiences between and within ethnic minority groups in relation to higher education (Modood, 1993; Taylor, 1993a).

In this chapter we explore these issues of identity from the perspective of young South Asian women continuing with their education beyond the age of sixteen. These are important issues as they lay out a context for the sub-sequent chapters by outlining the identity positions from which the young women themselves talk about their educational experiences. We explore a variety of dimensions of identity, especially ethnicity, religion, Britishness and how the young women feel that they belong to and express these identities, for example through styles of dress. We begin with a comparison of ethnic identities in terms of how far and in what ways the young women describe themselves as Bangladeshi, Indian or Pakistani, and how these sources of identification relate to ideas of Britishness and religious identities.

Bangladeshi identities

The main themes of the young Bangladeshi women's self-understandings of their ethnic identities encompass language, food and clothing, personality and behaviour. For example, according to Zarqa Aslam (a sixth-former in Leeds) being Bangladeshi for her means: 'Speaking in Bengali at home, eating my boiled rice and curry and we wear the traditional clothes as well. I help my mum at home too.' Often they talked about their personality and their culture in a way that emphasised their ethnicity as an aspect of their self-identity and their personal behaviour, showing how ethnicity is a mutable practice. In these discussions relationships with parents are seen as important not only in terms of learning about cultural practices, but also in continuing to speak Bengali. In this sense the home and the role of women within it raising children, dressing appropriately, cooking food and taking up appropriate roles in key rituals such as weddings is central to the re-creation of ideas of ethnic distinctiveness for the women:

> Because of my personality and behaviour is more inline with my culture. And I feel more Bangladeshi than I do British ... the way I dress, I dress in *shalwar kameez* at home and on special occasions I wear saris, which is an identity of Bangladeshis. I speak Bengali at home. (Zainab Ali, graduate, Leeds)

> It is who I am, it is my culture ... My parents taught us what they know so my upbringing and culture is a result of that. But also through speaking Bengali, dressing in suits, eating Bengali foods and even the basics, just my name being Bengali allows me to identify with being Bengali. (Mussarat Begum, sixth-former, Leeds)

Furthermore, trans-national relationships and practices help to maintain a sense of ethnic distinction amongst the young Bangladeshi women. Rassool (1999: 30) has suggested that these trans-national connections help young ethnic minority people to have a sense of both their cultural origins and to reject aspects of dominant British culture that marginalise them. This shows how the idea of diaspora as a trans-national phenomenon works in practice. When talking about their visits back to Bangladesh and how these relate to their identities, two particular themes emerge from our interviews with the young Bangladeshi women. The first of these is that the very fact of there being trans-national contacts that are renewed through visits, and in some cases marriages, sustains a sense of ethnic self-identity:

> I speak the language, I live in an area where there is quite a large population of Bangladeshi people, I still follow a lot of the culture... I visit back home a lot, I have been married back in Bangladesh, my husband is pure Bangladeshi. (Jabeen Ahmad, undergraduate, Leeds)

Secondly, several women spoke of how when they visit Bangladesh they often feel more British than Bangladeshi. In this way their trans-national movements underline the idea that ethnic identity is contextual, rather than something fixed or primordial. In Britain their distinctiveness as Bangladeshis or as Muslims is highlighted for them by the wider society but, whilst they are visiting Bangladesh their identities and values as British citizens come to the fore. This contradicts Rassool's (1999) suggestion that young ethnic minority people might develop a sense of belonging to the country where their parents were born through travel to those countries. For some of the women who told us about negative aspects of their visits to Bangladesh, this leads them to reject certain aspects of what they see as Bangladeshi identity:

> The reason I kind of reject some parts of my Bangladeshi culture and when I go to Bangladesh I am not a Bangladeshi. That is the thing with us British Bengalis we are neither here or there. Because when you got over there you are treated completely different, because you have a British passport they worship the ground you walk on so you are not treated for you, you are treated for your citizenship. (Amina Chaudhary, graduate, Leeds)

> The culture that first and foremost around me and shapes me is the Bangladeshi values and the Islamic values and then it is the British values. But the British values are quite grey I think because, when you go to Bangladesh and you are talking to people and their ideologies, you realise that 'oh I am quite British really, my values and ideas are quite different from them'. And that comes from the English culture. (Fatima Begum, undergraduate, Leeds)

> The fact that I was born and bred here and totally different in the way I think the way I live my life is totally different to someone in Bangladesh, I went there eight years ago and I didn't really feel as though I was as similar to them there was a difference there was a gap between the way I did things, saw things and the way like my cousin was the same age so her outlook in life ... they're a lot more mature I think and they see things in a way my mum would. (Halima Akhtar, Bangladeshi graduate, Leeds)

Indian identities

The Indian women generally had to be probed more to think about the question of their ethnic identity. For example, Bina Mukherjee (an undergraduate in Leeds) defined herself as being British Indian, with her Indian heritage defined in terms of language: 'British Indian, because I was born here and I haven't been to India but I speak Gujarati'. For these young women there were often clear boundaries drawn between their British identities and their ethnic identities:

> I'd probably say British I would because I was born here. I can speak English, go out clubbing and stuff. I still go to the temple do *dawa*, eat with your hands other than that I mean I don't know. I've been to India twice since I was born. (Anisha Patel, undergraduate, Leeds)

> Eat Indian food, wear Indian dress to some extent, speak Gujarati, speak the Indian language ... I would appear more Indian than I do British no matter what I wear, but I feel British Indian I guess. (Saudah Shah, graduate, Leeds)

There were also Indian women who were extremely proud of their Indian ethnicity. This entails a sense of belonging to their parents' origins, and this is maintained through visits to India, as well as the consumption of Bollywood films in the way suggested by Rassool (1999). For these women, the family, its values and its origins are a key source of ethnic self-identification:

> I've got a British passport but I'm Indian. I would never say that I'm English because I'm not. I think that's really important and I don't want to be English. It wasn't easy having one foot in English society and the Indian, but a lot of people I meet say they can tell I'm very Indian and that's not because I speak with a strong accent or something, because my family are important to me and I've been back to India and I want to go again and I like watching Bollywood films and because that's who I am, that's where my roots are. That's where my parents are from and it's so important to me to pass that on to my children to know that you're Indian and be proud of it and don't aspire to be something that you're not. (Davinder Kaur, undergraduate, Leeds)

However, in contrast to this pride in Indian origins some of the young women did not like the term Indian, and they preferred non-national forms of identification associated with the part of India that their parents migrated from or their religion. In this way they were resisting the dominant definitions of their identity and origins:

> If someone said to me 'What are you?' I would probably say 'Indian'. But I don't really like the word Indian. You don't talk Indian do you? No you talk in Punjabi or Hindi or Urdu, you don't talk Indian. India is a place. I don't like the word Indian. But then Asian is a bit like that because I have really pale skin so people say 'Well which

part' and I say 'India, is it not obvious?' If someone were to describe me I would like them to say I was a Punjabi girl or a Sikh girl who is born in the UK ... because it is my culture. (Simi Banu, Undergraduate, Leeds)

Pakistani identities

The young women from Pakistani backgrounds talked about their ethnic identities in a variety of ways. They often linked their parents' national origins with cultural practices, language and their religion as Muslims. There is some evidence of and overlapping with Indian identity through the consumption of Bollywood movies, but this really signifies the way in which Bollywood output appeals to a pan-ethnic South Asian audience. They also discussed the distinctive significance of family life, speaking and using Punjabi or Urdu with other family members and friends, and some of them mentioned their on-going contacts with Pakistan. Also, as suggested by Rassool (1999), visits to Pakistan sometimes developed a stronger sense of identification with their parents' origins. The expectation that some of had of marrying someone from Pakistan heightened for them the need to identify with the country of their parents:

> It's important in a sense that it's where my roots lay, and it's where my parents are born, which is the most important connection with Pakistan, and I recently went to Pakistan last year, and I found myself reading up about it a lot more ... We eat Pakistani food, I learned to cook Pakistani food. I do like to wear Pakistani dress but I prefer sari's which is more Indian I suppose, but I quite like the *shalwaar kameez* – not so much the shalwaar, but I do the kameez a lot, because I quite like the style. In terms of language – my-sister-in law speaks Urdu so I speak Urdu with her and my parents. (Hikmat Bibi, undergraduate, Leeds)

> I suppose the language I speak, especially at home and I have links to Pakistan because it is where my parents are from ... I think it is important to have links there because you don't know; I might get married to someone from there. (Shanaz Ali, sixth-former, Leeds)

> Well I'm from Pakistan my parents are from there. Our culture is totally different to any other and I really like it. Although I wear English clothes but at home I don't wear them. I wear them here because to feel part of every thing else. I speak Punjabi but mostly we speak English at home. (Rafika Amin, sixth-former, Leeds)

> I do think it's a good thing to know your roots and know your cultural heritage so being Pakistani and kind of Muslim heritage is important because it kind of helps me understand my parents better, the way they have been brought up and the kind of values that they have and the ideals that they have been brought up with. I think in that respect it's very important to know your roots and where your parents are from and what kind of upbringing they've had before you. (Nargis Khan, graduate, Leeds)

Some of the young Pakistani women rejected aspects of what they saw as Pakistani culture. However, rather than embracing a British identity, more emphasis was given by these women to their Muslim identities. Also important here were their experiences of visits to Pakistan where, in a similar way to the Bangladeshi women, their distinction as British citizens was raised:

> A lot of the Pakistani-ness, is the cultural side of it. And there are a lot of things in my culture, not in my religion that I don't accept, and never have accepted, and I still don't accept, so if I was to say I'm Pakistani – that's like a cultural thing, it's not a religious thing. If you go to Pakistan, and you compare the way that we think here, and the way that they think there, you'd realise how different you are. It's not something that I used to be that I'm not any more. It's not the fact that I'm educated now so all of a sudden I'm not Pakistani – it's not even an educated or non-educated thing – it's the cultural thing. (Parveen, graduate, Leeds)

> I just don't really identify with it. I don't really relate to it ... Just because my parents are from Pakistan and a lot of my relatives are still over there I wouldn't call myself a Pakistani. I wear Asian clothes and eat Asian food. I haven't been brought up there or lived there so I can't say that I relate to their values or how they seem themselves or associate with others because, well I haven't even been there so it's hard for me to relate to them or consider myself Pakistani. (Ambiya Siddique, graduate, Leeds)

Muslim identity

When the young women were asked about their identities, we have seen how they often talked about themselves being British and Pakistani, Bangladeshi or Indian. However, for those who are Muslims they also talked extensively about their religious affiliations. The Muslim women largely defined themselves in terms of a multi-fold identity, in the form of a three-part identity: Muslim, British and Bangladeshi, Indian or Pakistani. According to Alpha Rehman for example, she immediately replied 'I am Muslim, British Bangladeshi'. This was a common form of response amongst the Muslim women, and supports other research on the way in which religious identity is increasingly significant for young British Muslims (Jacobson, 1997; Samad, 1996). Islam is seen as more important to many of the young Muslim women because it plays a more central role in regulating their daily lives. It is also seen as a broader yet more fundamental source of identity than ethnicity. Some aspects of ethnicity they perceive as being in conflict with Islamic values:

> If anyone really just asks me I just say Muslim ... the way I dress, how my day is planned, a lot of what I say, a lot of what I do ... you have the five days of prayers, so all my day would be planned around them and I would make sure I am able to complete them. So my whole day would revolve around these. And so it is all planned alongside that and in what I do. (Zahra Amin, Bangladeshi sixth-former, Leeds)

Muslim identity comes first, that is what I am then it my Pakistani and British identity ... it kind of acts as a uniting kind of thing me as a Muslim. It is what I am in terms of my religion and is more important than my cultural identity. Going round saying I'm a Pakistani is more restrictive, I probably wouldn't open up to more people, but saying I'm a Muslim I have really good Arab friends and other Muslims who I have met through being Muslim first and then the others later. (Shameem Khan, Pakistani undergraduate, Leeds)

Well my religion is like Muslim so I've been brought up to read the Quran and stuff like that. I think us Muslims now we have western side to us when we're with our friends and when we go home we have Asian side. I think there two identities. I'll describe myself as British Muslim then. (Sajida Sabir, Pakistani sixth-former, Leeds)

At first I would define myself as a Muslim first and British and then Bengali. Reason for that is because even though I am from a Bangladeshi background and even though my roots are Bangladeshi I still think that my religion is the most important thing. My Bengali culture is very culturally orientated and it imposes a lot of ideas and thoughts that our religion does not agree with. Because our ancestors originally were Hindu and sometimes especially our older generation they get caught up with what you are supposed to do and what you are not supposed to do. But in our religion it states what is right and what is wrong. (Amina Chaudhary, Bangladeshi graduate, Leeds)

Some of the women defined themselves solely as Muslims, and sometime they used this to distinguish themselves from their parents who they felt had a more ethno-national sense of identity. These generational differences echo Jacobson's (1997) arguments about the ways in which young second-generation Pakistani Muslims distinguish between religious identity and ethnic identity:

I'd just say I was a Muslim ... that is my being, that's what I follow, that's my life basically so I read my prayers five times a day, as much as I can. My thinking is Muslim thinking rather than Pakistani. Because to say Pakistani, just to say Pakistani is very traditional, because my parents have a very Pakistani thinking I'd say. I wouldn't say that they have as much Islamic thinking as their children have now. (Farhana Sheikh, Pakistani sixth-former, Leeds)

Some of the young Muslim women described to us how their Muslim faith had grown stronger over time. In particular when they moved on to college or university they came into contact with other Muslims, or had facilities to pray regularly during the daytime. At university they often had the first opportunities to learn about Islam away from the oral culture of their parents. There were also some women whose home life had less of a religious influence, but being away from home they had learnt more and were engaged in religious activities for the first time:

At college to be honest, at the time when I was at college I wasn't praying as much. So now that I'm here hopefully if I start doing the course I'm going to make sure they have that facility for us Muslims because it's something they should have. (Farhana Sheikh, Pakistani sixth-former, Leeds)

I don't pray much but I do really want to pray say it all the time to the girls in the house just recently found out there's a gathering that happens at the mosque all like Muslim women every Sunday but I wanted to go every Sunday and I went home one weekend and brought some Asian suits up. My mum started laughing she's like are you alright is your head alright I said no I want to go every Sunday it's at 2 o'clock I've not been yet we've just found out recently like a few months ago I do want to go I have intention every week. There's me and Amina that are Muslims in the house it's quite hard because she's in her third year she hasn't had time at all and I don't want to go on my own not somewhere I've not been before. (Jasmin Ali, Pakistani undergraduate, Leeds)

Britishness and its hybrid forms

There were several ways in which the young women identified themselves as British. The first of these we call hybrid Britishness, where they explicitly selected those aspects of what they saw as British culture that were compatible with their South Asian culture or religion. Secondly, they identified themselves as British citizens because they were born in Britain. Thirdly, they identified Britishness with speaking English as their main language. Fourthly, some of the young women identified Britishness with certain political and cultural values that they saw themselves as expressing or articulating. Finally, some of the young women saw Britishness as a white identity that actively excluded them. This is an analytical typology, and many of the women talked about more than one of these dimensions when discussed how British they felt that they were. Many of the young women referred to how vague and imprecise British identity can be. For example, Zainab Ali (Bangladeshi graduate, Leeds) told us: 'It's vague thing I really don't know what makes me British.' Others often referred to what they saw as British cultural practices in terms of leisure or food:

I suppose I do go to the cinema with my friends and that's something different, I get together with my friends. We go out together for lunch but don't always think about fish and chips, we might think about having a Yorkshire pudding! (Sobia Ali, Bangladeshi graduate, Leeds)

The idea of hybrid Britishness is perhaps most simply expressed when many of the young women described themselves as British-Bangladeshi or British-Muslim, for example. When asked to describe what this meant to them, the young women talked about how they identified with certain cultural or political aspects that they felt were compatible with their South Asian culture or, often in the case of Muslims, their religion:

> I define British my way not the normal definitions given to it. Like I have taken on the good points of Britishness which don't conflict with our religion or culture and left all the bad points. Like we have gone in the system of education, am aware of the politics here. I enjoy fish and chips so I guess that's British in a way. (Tahira Safder, Pakistani graduate, Leeds)

> I'm trying to balance both I was brought up here so obviously I picked up western bit of what I think is best, best thing being here is you can pick and choose. I can practise my religion and also I can the best bit of western culture I can pick that as well and I think I've got that so I think I'm balanced in both. (Zoreena Bibi, Bangladeshi graduate, Leeds)

Identifying themselves as British citizens was very important to some of the young women. This arises because they identify very strongly with the country where they were born and where they have grown up. This also entails for them speaking English and adhering to its laws:

> I have lived here all my life and I do not really know Bangladesh but because of my parents I have only been to Bangladesh twice and I do not really know anything about it ... If I lived in Bangladesh then obviously I would say I am Bangladeshi and because you are here and you are British, it is not because you do something that is British. It is because you just live there and it is called Britain and you are British. (Zahra Amin, Bangladeshi sixth-former, Leeds)

> Cos I was born here, my passport's British that's my identity over here I don't have a Pakistani passport so it's based on that. (Saiqa Ali, Pakistani sixth-former, Leeds)

> I was born in this country, I speak the language, I follow the rules and the regulations of the country I do everything probably that all the British people do, and I've got a British passport. (Jabeen Ahmad, Bangladeshi undergraduate, Leeds)

The issue of speaking English as being essential to British identity was a question raised by politicians in response to the riots in the North of England in 2001 (Bagguley and Hussain, 2006; Cantle, 2001; Denham, 2002). It is therefore interesting to note that a number of the young women raised speaking English as a dimension of their sense of Britishness. However, we are not able to probe into the origins of this linguistic sense of identity to see how far they felt that they were influenced by the wider political debates about the role of English as an aspect of British identity. The introduction of speaking English in the interviews was often done by the young women in the context of a list of wider cultural attributes and practices that they regarded as British, such as wearing western clothes, as well as just residing in Britain:

Well I'm living here and I speak English fluently and it is also the way we think and live really, because if we were in Bangladesh it would be a very different way of living ... I eat fish and chips ... I watch TV a lot and yeah, going out to the park and going out with friends to the cinemas. (Zarqa Aslam, Bangaldeshi sixth-former, Leeds)

I dress British, I eat British food I speak English. I live in Britain. Have a lot of British friends. I am a part of the British social life. (Priya Chopra, Indian sixth-former, Leeds)

Well the language makes me British, I have no language problems I can speak English. I suppose that I can live in this country without any problems. (Adiba Kamran, Pakistani graduate, Leeds)

To the extent that I was born here, brought up here. In the extent of everyday life, speaking in English, participating to a certain extent in the British society. Participating in the education system. Wearing English clothes. (Miriam Patel, Indian Muslim graduate, Leeds)

Some of the young women defined their Britishness in terms of what they saw as liberal cultural and political values. For example, Shahida Azam (an Indian undergraduate in Leeds) defined her British identity as being '... maybe the values I hold are very liberal are very British kind of values.' This identification with liberal values they often saw as arising from their education in Britain and living in this country, in contrast to their parents' identities:

I think I'm quite British in my thoughts definitely, in a sense that when my parents say things that are more Pakistani orientated ... that view doesn't make sense but that's from how they grew up, and me living in this country, has broadened my horizons in a way, it's not one specific, British mentality, but you can pick the goodness out of it and implement that really well. (Hikmat Bibi, Pakistani graduate, Leeds)

I think the higher up in the education system I am coming along, the more I'm taking on the western values ... the more English liberal view of things ... (Fatima Begum, Bangladeshi undergraduate, Leeds)

Many of the Bangladeshi and especially Pakistani Muslim women felt that although they were British in some sense, they also felt excluded by what Britishness has come to mean. This was explicitly linked to political developments since 2001, especially the responses to the 2001 attacks in the USA on New York and the Pentagon. Although these women identified themselves as British through their birth, their education and various aspects of their lives, they felt excluded from being fully British by the dominant culture:

I was born in this country but I don't feel that I could be British you see I don't feel a part of it ... It's because of the way that sometimes you do get treated different as well as what some people say is 'what are you doing in this country?' and everything and they give you that look and that's why ... it does stop you being a part of it cos people always look down on you and everything and treat you as though you don't belong here. (Nalufa Begum, Bangladeshi sixth-former, Leeds)

I feel British sometimes I don't feel English. I feel British yeah kind of yeah but not always I mean because there's like so much racism and stuff you feel that you're always an outsider but in that sense because of the things that you have in terms of your language and your outlook on life in terms of the values that you have they're very British anyway ... the fact that I was born British and that I have lived in the western culture British culture I've had an education in British schools, I work with British people and you know I do things obviously in the wider circle I think that very much makes me feel as though am British. I don't feel but only then do I feel a little bit like outcast when British white people don't consider me of me like Asian people as part of themselves. Only then does it like have an impact and you think like am different. And then do I realise that these people really don't consider me as a British. (Shabnam Yousaf, Pakistani undergraduate, Leeds)

I eat British, I speak British, I live British ... It's hard to kind of say how far are you a British person. I recently have not felt very British. After September the 11th I felt like I don't belong here anymore. I've seriously considered migrating over to Pakistan, living and working over there. I don't feel like I want to pay this government my taxes. I don't feel like I belong in this country. But that's not because I don't belong, more because people don't let me belong. (Samreen Patel, Pakistani graduate, Leeds)

Dress

The question of traditional dress for British South Asian Muslim women in public life became a hotly contested political issue towards the end of the writing of this book. A leading Labour Party politician, Jack Straw, suggested in his regular column for his local newspaper that he preferred women who wear the *niqab* or veil to remove it when they meet him at his surgery as it facilitates communication. The debate which followed saw the majority of politicians agreeing with Straw, and public support for him in opinion polls (*The Guardian*, 6 October 2006). This was closely followed by reports of a classroom assistant in a school in Dewsbury contesting her dismissal for refusing to remove her *niqab* when male staff were present in the classroom (*The Guardian*, 25 November, 2006). At the end of 2006, it was even suggested erroneously that one of the suspects in the murder of PC Sharon Beshenivsky in Bradford had escaped from the country by using his sister's passport and wearing a *niqab*! (*The Guardian*, 20 December 2006). These incidents have more than ever before politicised the question of what British South Asian Muslim women wear, and follow upon a longer series of public political conflicts between Muslims and the rest of British society over the question of the wearing of *hijab*. Their dress is now taken as a powerful signifier of community cohesion versus segregation, and even seen as representing support for political violence such as the 2005 London bombings (Werbner, 2005). Consequently, whether they like it or not, what to wear for British South Asian women is no longer simply a question of aesthetics, comfort or expression of ethnic or religious identity, it is seen as a political decision in the eyes of others.

The role of South Asian traditional dress for women has been the subject of previous research a number of times (Anwar, 1998: 144-7; Drury, 1991; Dwyer, 1999b; Modood *et al*, 1997: 326-8; Shain, 2003). Central to this work has been an exploration of generational differences, the role of dress in repressing South Asian women and the greater conservatism of South Asian Muslims in matters of dress for women. Some of this literature has been concerned with how far the wearing of traditional Asian clothing was the choice of the women or if they were forced to do so by their parents (Drury, 1991; Shain, 2003). However, rights to wear traditional dress, particularly *shalwar kameez* and the *hijab* for South Asian and Muslim women have also been major questions for equal opportunities legislation and policies (Modood *et al*, 1997: 326). Furthermore, these traditional forms of dress mean that South Asian Muslim women are more likely to be readily identified as Muslims and subject to attack and harrassment on that basis.

Modood *et al* (1997) were the first to document the extent to which South Asian people wear Asian clothes. They found that most South Asian women wear Asian clothes at some point, but that most South Asian men do not, and that Bangladeshi and Pakistani women were most likely to wear such clothing most of the time. The workplace was where they were least likely to wear Asian clothes, although almost all Bangladeshi and Pakistani women did so at home or at social events such as weddings. Young women in particular were more likely to wear Asian clothes some of the time. Attitudes towards Asian clothes have also been explored by Anwar (1998: 144-7), and he found that young people were more likely to approve of Asian women wearing Western clothes.

However, subsequent political and cultural developments suggest that the situation is now more complex than suggested in previous literature (Dwyer, 1999a; Shain, 2003). Central to this is the apparently increased preference amongst South Asian Muslim women for wearing the *hijab* (a more complete head covering) as opposed to the *dupatta* (a loose head scarf typically worn with *shalwar kameez*). This is furthermore associated with a re-assertion of Muslim identities in the currently highly hostile political environment. Thus the *hijab* and the *niqab* have been reclaimed by Muslim women as signs not of male control over their bodies, but as symbols of religious expression, resistance to Islamophobia and US and British military interventions in Afghanistan and Iraq (Werbner, 2005). This is not to deny the significance of male constraints on South Asian women's lives, but to recognise that these women are not entirely passive and powerless either (Dwyer, 1999a). However, what all of this literature emphasises is the way in which many young South Asian women, Muslim and non-Muslim, wear a variety of clothes in different contexts, thus expressing their skills as cultural navigators (Ballard, 1994).

There were three approaches to traditional dress amongst the young women that we interviewed. Firstly, those who wore traditional dress all the time; this was often linked to a stronger sense of religious and cultural identity. Secondly, those who wore traditional dress only on special occasions such as weddings, visits to the temple, etc. These women also often wore traditional dress when they were at home. This was often to reassure their parents that they were maintaining their respect for their parents' culture. They wore what they defined as western dress the rest of the time at university or work. Thirdly, there were those who only wore traditional dress when they decided to wear it. This last category often wore traditional dress when the weather was suitable.

Nearly all the respondents wore western dress; the only ones who wore solely traditional dress were Pakistani, none of the Indian women who were interviewed wore traditional dress all the time and talked about only wearing such clothes at home or on special occasions. Many of the Bangaldeshi, Pakistani and Indian Muslim women automatically explained the way in which they dressed as being an expression of their religious beliefs. This was the case even if they were wearing western-style clothing, which typically entailed wearing jeans or trousers in combination with the *hijab*.

Those who wore traditional Asian dress all the time often did so as an outward expression of their religious or ethnic identity. For some this also entailed being a role model for other South Asian Muslim women, and resisting some of the pressures of living in a predominantly non-Muslim culture. Rahila Akhtar, an Indian Muslim graduate, wears what she sees as traditional Islamic dress:

> I wear the full *hijab* I cover my face as well I wear the *niqab*. I work in a Muslim school so that's quite important cos I do the morning seminars every day two days

51

a week so I lecture them in how to be a good Muslim especially when you're living in this country especially the teenagers they've got lots of pressures on them, peer pressure, under pressure so you let them know what bit is best.

Rizwana Ali (Pakistani sixth-former, Leeds) wears traditional dress to maintain her sense of ethnic and religious identity. For her it is important not to feel pressurised into wearing Western style clothes by the wider society:

Just because I live here and go to school here it doesn't mean I have to be like everyone else. Everyone is still different at the end of the day. Just because I live here I don't totally have to follow what they do, I still have to remember my roots.

The second category of dress strategy was where women wore traditional dress on special occasions, or only when they were at home. They had clear ideas about when they wore traditional Asian clothes, and gave their reasons. Their explanations often concerned respect for older members of their family or community. But others genuinely enjoyed wearing traditional Asian clothes:

When I'm going out like to work or to sixth form or anything I wear trousers and everything and when I'm at home I wear traditional clothes ... it's just respect for my parents I think as well and to show them that I haven't forgotten my culture and things like that ... (Nalufa Begum, Bangladeshi sixth-former, Leeds)

When you're at home you feel more comfortable wearing *shalwaar kameez* than trousers and stuff because you have all your mum's friends and all these men coming in and out and trousers are not really appropriate when you're at home when you've got all these people coming around, especially if you've got your uncles coming and they're looking at you thinking 'what the hell is wrong with her?' (Jameela Yaqoob, Bangladeshi undergraduate, Leeds)

I wear my Asian suits when I have to when I go to weddings or if I'm going to some elderly people's houses and I don't feel shy or embarrassed at all I love wearing Asian suits I do like to pray and I love *Eid* festivals I love them I would like leave everything here and go back home for it even though I have spend an *Eid* here once on my own but I love all my cultural things I love weddings and love getting involved all the traditional things. (Jasmin Ali, Pakistani undergraduate, Leeds)

Finally, there were those who chose what they wore according to circumstances or comfort. Here the rules of dress seemed more flexible, although the young women often still articulated a sense of wearing clothes that were appropriate to the setting such as work or weddings. According to Meena Devi, an Indian undergraduate: 'I wear western and traditional like when I got to weddings and temple ... I just dress however I feel like dressing.' Many of the Bangladeshi and Pakistani Muslim women also expressed similar ideas about choosing what they wore to suit the situation:

Well you see it a long top with jeans. The only reason why I am wearing that is because I've got to go to work and after work I'm going out you see from work; so I have dressed up a bit. So that is the only reason why I am wearing this, other than that I wear *shalwar kameez* ... I wear trousers but long tops, so that they cover my bottom. I wear *shalwar kameez*, I have worn it several times to university and I have worn it to work. I wear a mixture of both types of clothes. (Shameem Khan, Pakistani undergraduate, Leeds)

I don't always wear *shalwar kameez* and I don't always wear trousers, I wear both really, but I do think I wear more trousers and skirts. I don't always wear traditional dress at home; I wear trousers at home as well. It is only sometimes when I want to ... my mum says I look better in *shalwar kameez*, so I don't know she says that may be because she wants me to wear more *shalwar kameez*. (Saira Begum, Bangladeshi sixth-former, Leeds)

It's just something that I feel comfortable in because I'm at home but when I'm at work I wear trousers and a jumper and things like that ... As long as I cover myself then that's fine they (her parents) are okay with it ... If I was going out with my friends I would wear something English like trousers or something like that so it's different. (Sobia Ali, Bangladeshi undergraduate, Leeds)

A particular theme of some earlier research into the styles of dressing of South Asian women has been how far their choice of dress was constrained by their parents (Drury, 1991; Shain, 2003). We did not encounter any instances of young women with strong feelings that they had a lack of choice about how they dressed. However, the Muslim women often referred to the expectations of the older generation, but how these were often flexible accommodating western styles of dress as long as they met with Islamic requirements for modesty. Within this broader religious context we found that the young women were able to exercise a considerable degree of choice and find pleasure in the diverse range of styles of dress available to them. Some of them, however, compared their relative freedom with the more limited choices available to some women in their communities:

Cos I like them I wear both I wear English as well. It's something I like really it's not something I'm imposed to wear it's like I feel more comfortable in them and I like the colours, Asian clothes are more like colourful whereas English clothes are not so ... My parents want me to be covered that's something they've always told me whatever you're wearing even if you're wearing Asian dress they are not allowed to be revealing whatever you're going to wear it's going to have to be covered then if it's covered it's alright something they say and also I agree with as well I can wear anything in any country, all comes to the dress sense as long as you're completely covered. (Aaliah Shah, Pakistani undergraduate, Leeds)

... my parents wanted to give me that extra freedom that extra choice, like you've got choice to wear *shalwar kameez*, you've got choice to wear skirt choice is there whatever you want to wear but with the rest of my family or the community that choice wasn't there and I don't think they could understand why my parents were letting me do that. (Faqrah Hamid, Pakistani graduate, Leeds)

Some of the Muslim women had experienced racist or islamophobic comments as a result of the way they dress. This is a different kind of constraint on their choices, as some of women had considered changing the way that they dress as a result of these experiences:

It's not always because of the skin colour it might be because of your religion. Because am a Muslim and I cover myself with my clothes and wear a scarf so I look different stand out from the group. Whereas if there was somebody Sikhs or Hindus who dress exactly like them they might not feel anything different. (Adiba Kamran, Pakistani graduate, Leeds)

I was walking down and someone just goes to me you Paki, you smell, you shouldn't have seen how angry I got it's so horrible ... I felt right awkward when it happened I thought do I smell that's why I changed the way I dressed I use to wear trousers and shirts and then I thought no I'm not going to wear it because I don't want to look too tp but I've now realised it's me I'm Asian I'm Pakistani if you don't like me do one and if you're going to be racist that's you not me. (Fozia Khanum, Pakistani sixth-former, Leeds)

Conclusion

In this chapter our approach to understanding the identities of young South Asian women continuing into further and higher education has been grounded in recent theoretical developments and empirical research around new ethnicities, diaspora and hybridity. This has enabled us to explore the complexity of the subject positions from which they are entering university and graduating in more detail and with attention to greater diversity than previous work.

Amongst the Bangladeshi women it is very clear that ethnic identity is experienced and expressed in a highly gendered way. Although they do not think about their ethnicity in an ethno-national way they do often emphasise their trans-national connections and speaking Bengali. The Indian women had a more abstract and diffuse sense of being Indian. For some their parents or grandparents' origins in a particular part of India was more important as a source of identity. The ways in which the Pakistani women talked about their ethnic identity was more similar to the Bangladeshi women than the Indian women.

Ethnicity acquires meaning in a highly gendered way through the ethical and moral dimensions of family life as symbols of ethnic distinctiveness. As others have noted previously, ethnic identity is bound up with the moral identities of women. Furthermore, language, such as speaking Punjabi or Urdu, is also an important dimension of identity as are the types of food they eat at home. Whilst practical connections with their parents' or grandparents' country of birth is important for some in re-affirming their diasporic sensibilities, for others visits to Bangladesh, India or Pakistan served to underline their hybridised identities as British-Asian women.

We found Islam and the idea of a Muslim identity to be especially important to the Bangladeshi and the Pakistani women, reflecting other research in this area (Jacobson, 1997; Samad, 1996). Like many second and third-generation Muslim migrants from the Indian sub-continent, they now identify more strongly with their religion than with some kind of ethno-national origin. British identity was also important for the young women and here the themes of citizenship, language and the wider political culture of Britain was what they identified with, although many of the Muslim students and graduates often felt excluded by white Britishness.

Dress was a complex area of the expression of ethnic and religious identity for the young women, one that has subsequently become highly politicised. Most of the women wore traditional South Asian dress at some point, with Muslim women who wore the *hijab* often combining it with western styles in a visible expression of cultural and religious hybridity. However, wearing traditional dress also carried with it certain risks for the women, especially the Muslims, as this makes them a highly visible ethnic and religious minority who could be subject to discrimination and harassment.

These issues are important as they concern the identity positions from which the young women approach higher education and experience life at university. As we shall see in the following chapters, their identities are central to their positions within their communities, and how these positions are changing, both as a result of their own education, and as a result of wider social, cultural and political forces. For example, later chapters will show how family life and community expectations shape which subjects they choose and whether or not they remain at home whilst studying at university. Their ethnic and religious identities and how they are expressed through their dress affect their experiences of racism and Islamophobia, both generally in the media and most immediately at school, in public places and at university.

4

Deciding to go to University

I n this chapter we look at the influences on young South Asian women's decisions about their education after the age of 16. There have been a number of recent studies that have considered how students make choices about going to university (Archer *et al*, 2003; Ball *et al*, 2002; Ball, 2003; Brooks, 2004; Connor, 2001; Morgan *et al*, 1999; Pugsley, 1998; Reay *et al*, 2005).

These have either relied upon models of consumer behaviour (Morgan *et al*, 1999), or emphasised the importance of class factors, whilst ethnicity and gender are seen as secondary. For example, they suggest that middle-class students assume that they will go to university, whilst those from working-class backgrounds and ethnic minorities are ambivalent and uncertain about this. Furthermore, it has been argued that only middle-class white parents play a central role in the choice of university by young people (Reay *et al*, 2005: 33). These studies often rely upon samples that make it difficult to examine specific questions about particular ethnic groups, and they tend to generalise in a rather vague way about ethnic minority groups.

A further theme of this recent research on young people's decisions about whether or not to go to university has been the apparent deterrent effect of the introduction of debt and fees (Callender, 2003; Callender and Jackson, 2004; Pennell and West, 2005), and we consider these issues in a later chapter. However, discussions of South Asian women's choices and decisions about university (for example, Ahmad, 2001) do not seem to have been influenced by this mainstream literature.

We begin by looking at the social class and educational background of the parents of the young women whom we interviewed. This enables us to see how far they differ from the national picture of the class background of South Asian women going to university around this time, as well as how far our sample differs from other recent studies. Furthermore, many explanations of success in entering university emphasise the importance of class factors, either in terms of the occupational backgrounds of the parents of university undergraduates (Halsey *et al*, 1980) or, more recently, the cultural and social capital of parents (Reay *et al*, 2005). In addition, some have suggested that there are distinct middle-class strategies for social mobility that encompass plans for a university education (Ball, 2003; Devine, 2004).

It is widely known from previous research that class background and the educational qualifications of parents influences the educational outcomes of their children in terms of access to university (Blackburn and Jarman, 1993; Egerton and Halsey, 1993; Halsey *et al*, 1980; Reay *et al*, 2005). Furthermore, we know that the different South Asian ethnic groups have different social class profiles and experiences of education (Modood *et al*, 1997). For these reasons, we begin this chapter with a detailed discussion of the class backgrounds of the young women whom we interviewed.

We go on to consider the young women's choice of A levels or vocational qualifications. These are important decisions, as others have suggested that the concentration of some ethnic minorities on vocational qualifications may disadvantage them in the competition for a university place. Recent research on how universities treat vocational qualifications (Connor *et al*, 2006) suggests that some admissions tutors believe that those applicants with vocational qualifications would be less able to succeed at university. Consequently those offering vocational qualifications when applying to university are often required to obtain higher tariff points than those offering A levels (Connor *et al*, 2006: 48).

In the following section we examine the main reasons for deciding to go to university. Large-scale surveys of ethnic minority groups in higher education have found that South Asians tend to emphasise employment prospects and family encouragement as key reasons for going to university (Connor *et al*, 2004: 27). This has also been found in some qualitative studies of South Asian women (Ahmad *et al*, 2003).

We then examine the influences on the young women's decisions to go to university. This is an important first step, particularly for young women from those communities where women have not previously entered higher education in the past in large numbers. Finally we look at the influences on their choice of qualification and subject. In this sense we are analysing the qualitative data in order to seek out possible explanations for some of the more striking statistical trends that we have uncovered.

There is an increased demand for higher education among South Asian women, one that has grown much more rapidly than among white women. One feature of the statistical data was that it showed that South Asian women studied subjects at university leading to traditional professions or that had a distinctive vocational element. Where relevant, we note differences between graduates, current undergraduates and those in the sixth form, as well as differences between ethnic groups and between Muslim and non-Muslim students.

However, before considering these issues we briefly summarise the class and educational background of the women's parents by way of providing an overview of the sample of young women that we interviewed.

Higher Education and social class backgrounds
Figure 4.1 provides details on the women's fathers' educational backgrounds in terms of whether or not the fathers had been to university, and here we distinguish between experience of UK and non-UK universities. This distinction is important in two ways. Firstly, non-UK qualifications are often not recognised by British employers and institutions, so that migrants with these qualifications may have experienced downward mobility compared to the occupations they might have held in their country of origin (Modood *et al*, 1997: 141-2). Consequently, the job level may actually obscure experience of and positive attitudes towards higher education (Modood, 2005: 302).

Figure 4.1

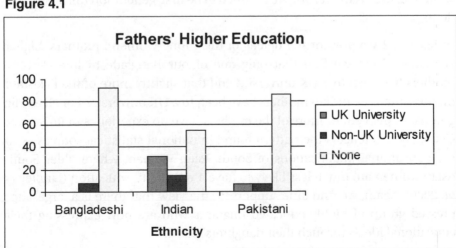

Figure 4.2

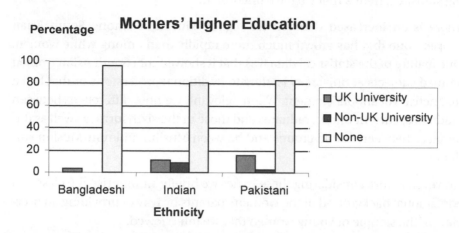

None of the women in our Bangladeshi sample had fathers who had graduated from a British university. Fewer than ten per cent of the Pakistani women we interviewed had fathers who had attended a British university. In contrast, more of the Indian women's fathers had experience of the UK university system, with around 30 per cent having graduated from a university in this country. A clear majority of both Bangladeshi and Pakistani fathers have not been to university either in the UK or elsewhere, whilst almost half of the Indian fathers have done so. Although our data is necessarily limited due to the sample size, we find no strong evidence in support of Modood's (2005) point that there may be substantial numbers of highly educated but lowly employed parents. In terms of the father's higher education, the young women in our study were or are destined to be first-generation university students.

In figure 4.2 we present the details of the young women's mothers' higher education. Here we find that only one of our Bangladeshi interviewees' mothers has been to a UK university, and that slightly more of the Pakistani mothers than the Indian mothers have been to a UK university. For all ethnic groups, 80 per cent or more of the mothers have no experience of university. Generally this reflects the pattern found in national statistical sources as to the educational qualifications of South Asian women, where older South Asian women are much less likely to have a university education (Lindley *et al*, 2006). Again, we find little support for the view that there is a large, suppressed group of highly educated migrants who are now expressing their educational ideals through their daughters' plans.

Figure 4.3

Percentage

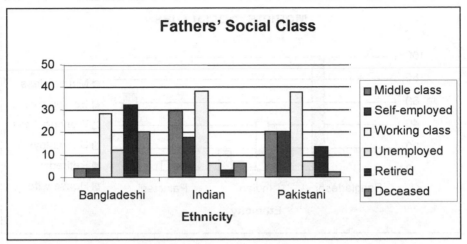

Regarding the social class background of our interviewees, the small size of our samples means that we have not been able to use any elaborate classifications of social class. Furthermore, in order to represent adequately the current economic circumstances of the women's families, we have included the categories of unemployed, retired and deceased. The middle-class amongst our sample were largely in professional and managerial occupations, the self-employed were almost entirely small family businesses that did not employ significant numbers of staff and the working-class are in largely semi-skilled and unskilled manual jobs.

Figure 4.3 provides details about the fathers' social class and economic circumstances. The Bangladeshi women overwhelmingly had fathers who were in working-class jobs, were retired or deceased. The fathers of the Indian women are mostly in employment of some kind. Almost a third are in middle-class jobs, almost a fifth self-employed and over a third in working-class jobs. The Pakistani fathers have a profile that falls somewhere between the Bangladeshi and Indian fathers. Over a third are in working-class jobs of some kind, with a fifth in middle-class employment or self-employed. Whilst some have suggested that the large proportion of those parents recorded in UCAS statistics as coming from unknown backgrounds in terms of social class are unemployed (Modood, 2005: 301), our data shows that they are very likely to be retired or, in the case of Bangladeshis, to be deceased.

Figure 4.4

Percentage

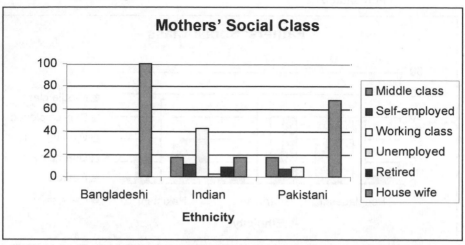

Finally, in this section we consider the mothers' position in relation to social class and economic activity in figure 4.4 above. This is especially important to consider, given the weight of research evidence that points to a significant difference for Bangladeshis and Pakistani women between the older generation's lack of participation in the labour market and the younger generation's increased labour market engagement (Dale *et al*, 2006; Lindley *et al*, 2006). Here we have added the category of housewife. None of the women reported that their mothers were deceased. All of the Bangladeshi women told us that their mothers were not in employment and were housewives. Over 60 per cent of the Pakistani mothers were housewives, but almost a fifth of them were in some kind of middle-class employment. In contrast to this, over 40 per cent of the Indian mothers were working in some type of working-class job, whilst less than a fifth were reported to be housewives. Here again, we found very distinct ethnically specific profiles of economic activity, and one that is largely reflected in official statistical sources and other recent studies (Dale *et al*, 2006; Lindley *et al*, 2006). There is no strong evidence that the young women's mothers are more engaged in employment than is generally the case for other women of the same generation from the same ethnic group.

The pioneers

Among those who had graduated were several women who had had older siblings who had gone through to university. However, besides this category were those who knew of pioneers – the first women within their families or even their local communities to go on to higher education. The Bangladeshi women in particular who had graduated were very likely to know the pioneers within their community. They were very often the first women within their family, and in several cases their wider community, to study at university. For example Fatima Begum, a Bangladeshi Law undergraduate in Leeds describes remembering that all the young women in her community ten or fifteen years earlier got married at the age of 16:

> My older sister who is 29 is from a different generation from me, she is seven years older than me but there is such a big difference between my sister and me. I remember when I was a kid, no girls went further than high school, and they had to go to high school because they would have the local services on to them asking them why you're truanting. They were expected to do well in education, you know to do well in your GCSEs, but at the end of your education system it meant that you were ready for marriage. I remember a lot of girls in my sister's time who got married at 16; they went to Bangladesh straight away in that summer and got married. I remember a lot of girls working in factories, sewing and that kind of thing. My sister and her friend Aisha were the only two Bengali girls in our community that went to college.

Having achieved their goal of studying for a degree, these pioneers acted in two ways. They were seen as role models for other younger women who wished to aspire to their position, thus the pioneers set the trend of going to university for younger South Asian women. The other role they performed was to be seen as deviant by some within their communities. Those within the wider community who had not educated their daughters perceived their education as deviating from the norm. For example, Amina Chowdhury, a Bangladeshi graduate, experienced much hostility from her community:

> I had a certain arrogance about my community because they did not believe in education. They did not believe women should study, even my aunty said what is the point of women studying there is no point because they are going to get married anyway and they are going to be a housewife.

Choosing qualifications

In this section we examine the influences on the choice of subject and the decisions about whether or not to do A levels or GNVQs. We find that the views of parents are extremely important in shaping the subjects chosen by the young women. Whilst studies of South Asian women and higher education have sometimes considered subject choice explicitly (Abbas, 2004; Ahmad *et al*, 2003), the more general studies of choice in relation to higher education (Reay *et al*, 2005) have often overlooked the issue of subject choice.

The role of parents in this process of subject choice in preparation for a university education has been found to be important for middle-class South Asians. In general it is felt that South Asian parents prefer their children to study subjects with a professional or vocational element (Abbas, 2004). Indeed, the quantitative data strongly suggests that young South Asian women are carrying out their parents' wishes, as we found in chapter 2 that they are concentrated in a few professional and vocational oriented subjects at degree level, albeit rather less than was previously the case.

Almost all of those in the sixth forms that we interviewed were pursuing a conventional route to higher education through A-levels. They are still the traditional path to higher education and were known to parents and the wider community as the most acceptable form of qualification. To some extent this contradicts the findings of some large-scale surveys which suggest that ethnic minorities disproportionately choose vocational qualifications (Connor *et al*, 2004: 16). Furthermore, it also contradicts the UCAS data on the qualifications studied prior to university by those who accepted degree places in 2001, the last year for which this data is available (see table 4.1 opposite). Of particular note is the fact that a significantly higher proportion of women from each of the South Asian groups than the white British category studied GNVQs prior to university. We suspect that this may have been an effect of the local opportunities and policies in the areas where we carried out the research, although we have no evidence to substantiate this.

In some instances, parents were very influential in choosing the A level route for their daughters. In other cases, the young women themselves had a clear view about the relative values of A levels and GNVQs for higher education. Consequently, few of the women followed less conventional routes such as GNVQs. As Pakistani sixth-former Fozia Khanum reveals, her decision to study A levels was following the advice she received from her family: 'They said do your A levels cos you can move on getting a good job and going to further education.'

Almost all of the young women currently at university had followed conventional routes through A levels and then on to degrees. These were defined by themselves as more conventional routes into higher education. Leena Mistry, an Indian currently at university, explained why from her point of view:

> I think A levels are more valued rather than vocational subjects and I think I just found it a straightforward way to get into uni ... if you do these different types of courses I think it might be more difficult to get in.

Table 4.1: Female Degree Acceptances 2001: qualification type by selected ethnic group

	Bangladeshi	Indian	Pakistani	White British
2+ GCE/VCE A Level passes	62.3%	68.0%	56.4%	67.7%
Access	3.4%	1.2%	3.1%	3.8%
Baccalaureate	0.0%	0.1%	0.0%	0.2%
BTEC/SCOTVEC	6.3%	5.1%	7.1%	7.2%
Deg/Partial Degree Credits	0.7%	1.5%	1.4%	1.5%
Foundation	0.9%	0.8%	0.5%	1.0%
GNVQ	16.7%	15.9%	18.5%	5.8%
None	4.7%	3.4%	4.8%	2.8%
Other	4.3%	3.3%	4.8%	2.8%
Scottish Highers	0.7%	0.7%	3.5%	7.2%
Grand Total	100.0%	100.0%	100.0%	100.0%

Source: UCAS

Many of the young women that we interviewed were highly critical of the careers advice that they received at school regarding their choices at age 16, especially those from Bangladeshi and Pakistani backgrounds. Many of them, for instance, were critical of the tendency to be offered only vocational qualifications by the teachers. However, they also recognised that many South Asian pupils whom they remember from school felt that vocational courses would be of more use to them in the labour market:

> Yeah, we had a careers centre. But tell you the truth, they were a bit crap they talked about NVQs a lot and I didn't want to do that I wanted to do A levels ... When I was in the education system most girls when they went on to the next level they didn't do academic A levels their next step was vocational. Now, few years below me, it is more standard to do A levels ... Because most of the students at my school were Asians, I don't know if they were giving that advice to the few minority white students. Most of the Asians though that is what they were interested in, the vocational; well that is what they went in to so it was more relevant to them ... The Asian students when I was at high school didn't have the interest, so they thought that if they didn't have the academic ability or interest to be doing anything at that level, it is best to be advising them at this level. (Fatima Begum, Bangladeshi undergraduate, Leeds)

Choosing subjects

For those still in the sixth form, irrespective of ethnicity, parents and families had a major role to play when choosing subjects at 16 and beyond. This reflects the findings in Abbas' (2004) study, for example. In some instances, the women were confident about asserting their own perspectives but ultimately abided by their family's decision. Families generally wanted their daughters to study traditional professional subjects such as law, medicine and dentistry; subjects such as sociology, English or psychology were not seen as serious academic disciplines. The underlying logic to this was the concern by the parents for their daughters' future employment prospects; parents wanted to ensure their child would be able to utilise their education to obtain work or for it to have value within the wider society. There were some women who were confident about parental support for their chosen subjects regardless of the parents' stated preferences. However, others were unhappy with their parents' preferences, and appeared to be successfully resisting these. According to Salima Azar, a Pakistani sixth-former, for example:

> My parents could tell me 'do medicine or law' but they know what I love is fashion so it would be pointless doing something else ... they know I wouldn't do as well if I did a different subject.

In contrast to this, others know they will be discouraged from their own wishes. For example, Hajra Khan, a Pakistani sixth-former who is repeating A levels, wanted to study beauty therapy, but she knows her mother will object to this choice:

> I wanted to do beauty therapy and that's something mum didn't approve of she said that's just a phase I'm going through that I want to do beauty. But it isn't it's a dream. But she's like you can do that afterwards. First get your degree and then do that.

However, in comparison to their certainty about the desirability of studying for A levels if they were thinking about going to university, many of the sixth-formers had not thought in any detail about which courses they would wish to follow at university. These uncertainties are very like those expressed in other studies by white working-class and ethnic minority sixth-formers (Archer and Hutchins, 2000; Reay *et al*, 2005). In some instances, their decisions about choice of subject were influenced by rather traditional ideas about their gender roles. For example Tahira Bibi, a Pakistani sixth-former, was choosing to do a course with a child-care component. She had decided upon this due to her domestic duties: 'I look after my cousin at home and I got all details so I thought child care would be good for me'.

Contrary to this general impression that there was a lack of thought and longer-term planning going into the choice of degree subjects, there were those who had seriously thought about their study and the implications of choosing specific subjects. Farhana Sheikh, a Pakistani sixth-former, talked about the religious reasons why she is choosing midwifery. This was a mature and thought out approach which contrasts with many in this age group:

> There is not a lot of Muslim midwifes. As a Muslim about to have a baby, I'd be happy knowing there is another Muslim sister helping me give birth than somebody who doesn't understand where I'm coming from.

Khalida Yousaf, a Bangladeshi sixth-former, explained her thinking about this as well, as she too wants to go into midwifery. However, she told us about the obstacles facing her in terms of convincing her parents about this decision. Her parents would have a very narrow view of what would be a suitable medical profession for her:

> They know it's a very different subject to go into for an Asian person cos Asians just want to be doctors or lawyers so when my parents tell people what I want to do they say 'why – has she gone crazy?' they think if you go to work in a hospital then you can only become a doctor and anything other than that there is no point.

The parents of those at university were also more likely to have encouraged them to study the more traditional subjects. For instance, according to Shahida Azam, an Indian Muslim currently at university studying broadcasting: 'you always get that pressure from family you should do engineer, doctor or lawyer, but I've just kind of ignored that cos I've been quite independent'. Many of the Pakistani women also expressed some resistance to their parents' preference for them to choose traditional professional subjects. For example, according to Shazia Manzoor her parents had always wanted her to study subjects that would lead to a career in one of the traditional professions instead of her preference for childhood studies: 'My mum wanted me to become a doctor or a solicitor 'typical' but I didn't want to be that because everybody was doing that.'

In choosing their own subject, some of the young women currently at university had faced objections from their parents. One such was Nina Patel, an Indian undergraduate who was studying law and communications. Her parents approved of the law aspect of her degree, but they do not like the communications element: 'judging from my family they have all gone into accountancy, pharmacy, dentistry'. Nina had to endure family's objections but was enjoying the course.

Similarly, parents object when their daughters change their minds about their degrees and their subjects from the more acceptable sciences or professional qualifications to humanities and social sciences. Aaliyah Shah, a Pakistani undergraduate, for example, studied initially for a psychology degree, but then transferred to Middle Eastern Studies, and her family were not happy, and told her it was a mistake because she could have become a psychologist. She does not regret her decision because, in her view: 'it's been a good degree really, cos I've got to know my religion more properly'.

Whilst some of the women went ahead with their own choices, there were others who were persuaded to do what their families had wanted, but now regretted it. The risk in cases such as these is that the students study subjects for which they may have neither the aptitude nor the enthusiasm and may therefore finish up with lower grades at A level or a lower class of degree upon graduation. Jasmine Ali's mother objected to her initial choice to do English, so she ended up studying Law. However, she now regrets that decision because she finds Law a difficult subject. She recalls her mother's reasoning as follows:

> She was like 'its going to be a better degree because its more recognised because its Law' and she was like 'with English language where are you going to get with it?' Law is one of the hardest degrees its on the top but I wish I'd done an easier degree.

There are, however, examples of women who have successfully resisted the pressures of their parents and are studying subjects of their choice. Simi Banu, an Indian undergraduate, decided to do English at university, a less conventional subject in the eyes of her parents. Simi was more concerned about enjoying a course than just doing something for the sake of her career and defends her decision to do English. Her father wanted her to become a pharmacist. Irrespective of the comments from others, Simi talks about her enjoyment of doing the course:

> I thought if I'm going to do a degree I would like to do it in something I enjoy. I don't want to force myself to study ... it was just what I wanted to do; I think I am one of the very few people who really enjoy their course. I never missed a lecture or a tutorial.

Interestingly though, some of the women chose the traditional professional and vocational subjects precisely because of the status that they would gain, and their longer-term labour market prospects. In cases such as this the preferences of the young women and their parents are in alignment with one another. Fatima Begum was one such young woman who chose Law because of the status it represents, and its potential for her as a career:

> It is stereotypes, you know that sounds good and it is going to make me sound good ... and also I wanted a career out of it ... I wanted it to be more purposeful than that, I wanted it to lead me to a career ... [my parents] put more preference and pressure on the stereotypically valued degrees like engineering, medicine and law ... at the end of the day what matters to them is getting the degree, so it doesn't matter what degree it is ultimately.

The encouragement to do well in education was emphasised by most of the young women that we interviewed. Many of them told us that their parents were keen for their child to progress well into higher education and this was continually stressed within the home. Such was the need for the parents to make sure that their child did well that some parents actually chose their daughters' subjects at A level and had an important input into their choice of degrees. Kalpana Bharati talked about her father choosing A levels which were impossible for her to pass. She did the subjects because her dad wanted her to become a professional:

> My dad said why don't you try doing these and then you can become a doctor or pharmacist, the typical Asian subjects but I don't know why I didn't do those in A levels because they weren't my stronger subjects.

Kalpana's father refused her the option of taking other routes, such as GNVQs, as A levels was his preferred route for her. However, this was to the detriment of Kalpana who found the chosen A levels extremely difficult. In her first year, Kalpana studied Biology, Chemistry, and Maths chosen for her by her father. She failed all three and retook her A levels. She was told to take, Computing, Maths, Business Studies and General studies, but failed again. She studied again at A level and this time took Business studies, Law, General Studies and AS levels in Statistics and ICT. Finally she managed to pass and eventually obtained a place at Leeds Metropolitan University to study Information Communication Management. Her choice of degree infuriated her father, but she had learnt not to attempt the subjects she was incapable of passing.

Situations of this kind may go some way to explaining why there are rather low levels of attainment among some Pakistani and Bangladeshi women at A level, as well as a high level of re-sits (Taylor, 1993b; Shiner and Modood, 2002).

Reflecting back, those who had graduated remembered that choosing subjects was sometimes problematic in the eyes of their parents; there were expectations for children to study traditional subjects. Sometimes, among those who had graduated, this had led to inappropriate decisions and careers. Jeevan Mudan, an Indian graduate, studied law as an undergraduate following the preferences of her parents. Having worked as a solicitor for almost seven years and being miserable in the process however, she had decided to go back to university for postgraduate study in sociology:

> I didn't chose the degree that I wanted to do I studied law because it's what my parents wanted me to study and I actually wanted to study sociology but there was a lot of pressure ... I think culturally people thought, my parents, siblings, thought my prospects were better with a law degree as opposed to sociology degree and I think they meant the occupational prospect was better ... they're the traditional safe sort of areas ... now I'm doing what I thought I wanted to do when I was about 18 and having another go at it really.

Whilst Jeevan felt under pressure, there were other women who argued successfully for their own preference. Samreen Patel, a Pakistani graduate, told us: 'I kind of battled with my dad, he wanted me to do medicine and I didn't'. She decided to pursue Law despite the fact that her father said it was a profession of 'lies' but she did so simply to assert her own autonomy: 'If I was going to go university then I wasn't going to do something that my dad wanted me to do ... I was going to do something that he hated.'

There are then a range of experiences in relation to the choice of subject. Whilst specialist research on South Asian women and higher education has broached this issue in the past (Ahmad *et al*, 2003), more general research on higher education choice (Reay *et al*, 2005) has almost entirely overlooked the role of parents in the choice of subjects by their offspring. Others (Abbas, 2004), however, have emphasised the central role that South Asian parents often have in the choice of subjects by their children. This is perhaps due to the fact that some South Asian parents have strong views and expectations about their children's choice of subjects in the sixth form and at university. These relate partly to the status of different subjects and the professional careers that they lead to, as in the case of law and medicine, but also relate to expectations about the marketability of different degrees and the need to obtain secure, well-paid employment as soon as possible after graduation.

We have also found that there is a strong preference for choosing A levels rather than vocational subjects, as these are seen by parents and young women as raising their chances of getting to university, especially one of the more prestigious institutions. This raises the issue of why so many South Asian students who go to university gain entry with vocational qualifications (Connor *et al*, 2004; 2006).

Firstly, we have seen that some women were guided by careers teachers towards vocational qualifications. Secondly, in the areas where our fieldwork was based, there are perhaps better options for A level study for South Asian women.

Whilst many parents still prefer their daughters to study subjects that would enable them to enter the traditional professions, this is not automatically translated into what the young women actually studied. Some accepted the route laid out for them by their parents and find it quite comfortable, whilst others change career after graduation. Others resist their parents' wishes to varying degrees either at A level, when choosing their degree or by changing their degree subject once they have been admitted to university.

Furthermore, there are a variety of reasons for studying particular subjects. Some take an instrumental view and study a subject that will quickly lead to a career with a good salary or high status within the community. This usually leads to a choice of a professional or vocational degree such as Law. Others, typically Muslims, are inspired by their religion to seek a career in a professional service where there is currently an under-representation of Muslims. This often leads to choosing a degree such as nursing or midwifery. Finally, there are those who have an enthusiasm for their subject and they often choose more traditional academic disciplines such as the humanities or social sciences.

To do a degree or not: reasons for going to university

All of the Indian students currently at university talked about higher education as being a natural progression from the sixth form. In this respect, they are very like the white middle-class students researched by others (Ball, 2003; Reay *et al*, 2005). Various aspects to this expectation arose from parents and the wider family as well as the school. Many of the young Indian women described how this was the assumption in their family:

> In my case everybody, all of my siblings had all gone to university and generally with outside of my family as well there was an assumption that everybody was going to go to university so I never saw it as an option it was just something that was going to happen ... (Jeevan Mudan, Indian graduate, Leeds)

Furthermore, the schools and colleges that they attended also seemed to assume that they would go to university. As Isha Sharma, an Indian undergraduate, told us: 'It's one of those things that is always drummed into you, not just from your parents but from school too'.

71

This assumption was also found in some of the Bangladeshi and Pakistani households, as Jasmin Ali, a Pakistani Muslim university student said, 'it wasn't even an option it's just like you're going to go to uni afterwards ... because you have older cousins and stuff you know you're going uni as well'. However, one further reason given for the strong parental support for higher education among some Bangladeshi parents was that they recognised that in Britain their daughters had opportunities for going to university that had been denied their parents. Jabeen Ahmad, a Bangladeshi Muslim undergraduate, explained: 'they haven't been educated back home they know an education for us here is important'. One important conclusion here is that early parental support and expectations were crucial for the decision to apply for university.

However, there is some diversity between ethnic groups. The Indian respondents often mentioned that expectations came from both the home and the school, but the Bangladeshis and Pakistani women tended to mention parental support alone, often in terms of taking up opportunities that the parents had not had. This confirms the findings of other studies have that focused on South Asian women and higher education (Abbas, 2004; Ahmad *et al*, 2003).

Some of the respondents talked about more instrumental economic reasons for going to university, as reported in national level surveys of students' reasons for going to university (Connor, 2001). There were a number of dimensions to this. For some it entailed simple social mobility; their university degree would enable them to obtain a better job. Obtaining a better job implied both a higher income and higher status in terms of respect from others. Another aspect of this was a sense of independence. Simi Banu, an Indian undergraduate, exemplifies this range of reasons:

> I hope to get a better job from it. I wanted independence. I wanted to live away from home. I wanted the lifestyle because my sister went to university she has this influx of money and she was in a massive city because we come from a very small town and I thought wow that really looks good and I really want to try it.

Among those expressing these kinds of instrumental economic reasons for choosing to go to university, this was often explained to us in terms of obtaining employment that was more highly paid. As Amina Khannum, an undergraduate Bangladeshi student in Birmingham, explained to us: 'I think I chose to go to university because I want to get a well-paid job, that was actually the point of going to uni – get a better paid job than I will with just A levels ...' Most of the women who spontaneously cited the improved prospects of a higher status job, a career and a higher income as their main reason for deciding to go to university were Bangladeshi and Pakistani:

> Because I believe that in this day and age you have to have some kind of education otherwise we will be stuck in clerical or admin jobs and that hasn't got a lot of money or anything like that so really it's about at the end of the day, whatever we do, it's always about money, you know so if you've got a good education and you've got good knowledge and everything you can educate your children then and the community and also you are seen as a role model so there are other people who will benefit from your knowledge and experience. (Jabeen Ahmad undergraduate, Bangladeshi, Leeds)

Some of the women wanted to pursue an education so that they could fulfil their parents' wishes. These desires on the part of parents are not just to obtain a degree, but are frequently expressed as a desire for their daughter to enter one of the established professions such as medicine or law. Fatima Begum, a Bangladeshi law undergraduate, explained this in the following way:

> My mum likes to call me a solicitor already, she goes 'oh yeah someone is training to be a solicitor'. Of all the children, my mum is the proudest of me in that sense, my mum values all their degrees but because I'm doing Law it's a bit different.

Others talked about the importance of education to their future role as parents and adult members of their own communities. This is an aspect of choosing to go into higher education that has perhaps been overlooked previously, and one that might be especially important for ethnic minority communities. According to Jabeen Ahmad, a Bangladeshi Muslim, one of the reasons that she gave for going on into higher education was that:

> If you've got a good education and you've got good knowledge you can educate your children then and the community and also you are seen as role model so there are other people who will benefit from your knowledge and experience.

There were some women who had a strong desire to learn, to study as an end in itself. In some respects this might be described as a traditional, middle-class reason for wanting to go to university. According to Fareena Anjum, a Pakistani graduate, it was a personal desire to study, and she goes on to describe in enthusiastic terms the sense of personal growth and independence that this has given her:

> It's a drive! Something drives you. Its like if I can pick up a book and think oh my god I'm really excited I really want to read this book, then I know I've got something inside me which is like pushing me ... I did my A levels I really enjoyed it, I loved doing all the work ... so I thought ok I feel ready for the uni life now, I'm a bit independent, I need to get a bit more and I can work on my own.

Other people who had been to university and acted as role models were important for most of the women that we interviewed. The most frequently cited role models were older sisters, cousins or friends of the family in the community. These role models were often important sources of information about how to apply to university, ideas for potential careers, as well as bargaining with reluctant parents. However, in a few instances such role models were not local but trans-national reflecting the increasingly impor-tance of higher education for women in South Asia. According to Shameem Khan, a Pakistani Muslim:

> My cousins even in Pakistan have all gone into further education they are either doing medicine or doing really good things and it is amazing really because you think we're sat here with all the opportunities that are available to us and they're sat in Pakistan, why not take these opportunities.

Thus there are a range of influences on South Asian women's decisions to go to university, and a variety of reasons for doing a degree. Of particular impor-tance was the support of parents, but also significant were role models and future employment prospects. Some respondents were also motivated by the desire for education as an end in itself, or to serve their own communities as adults.

The reasons given by the Indian women for deciding to do a degree clearly reflected their more middle-class and educated backgrounds. They were more likely to come from families where going to university was seen as the natural and normal progression after school. The Bangladeshi women in particular were more likely to give instrumental or economic reasons for go-ing to university. They had their eyes on their longer term careers, and obtain-ing better paid employment than their parents had been able to do. Pakistani women also often gave these longer term career goals as the reason for want-ing to go to university but, like some of the Bangladeshi women, they were also motivated to fulfil their parents' wishes, to take up opportunities that had been denied their parents as economic migrants, to study for reasons of self-fulfilment as well as contributing to their own communities.

Perceptions of different universities

Previous research on the choice of universities has emphasised the percep-tions and evaluations of different institutions by potential students (Abbas, 2004; Pugsley, 1998; Reay *et al*, 2005; Whitehead *et al*, 2006). These suggested that white middle-class applicants and their parents were acutely aware of the status of different institutions. Furthermore, Reay *et al* (2005) in particular argued that ethnic minority and working-class students were less conscious of the significance of the status of different universities. For ethnic minority students, Reay *et al* (2005: 127-8) suggested that the ethnic composition of a university's student body was key factor in whether or not they preferred that institution.

For the young South Asian women that we interviewed, their choices of institution are often in reality constrained by their parents' preferences for them to study locally, and we consider this in more detail in a later chapter. However, within this geographically constrained context the higher status red brick was often chosen over the local new universities. The prestige was recognised of Birmingham University or Leeds University, for example:

> Because it's got a really good reputation and its quite prestigious as well and I think it's a good university. It's convenient, it's close to home as well. And they had the course I wanted to do as well. (Khanez Mamood, undergraduate, Pakistani, Birmingham)

> I live in Birmingham so part that was the reason for me to come here. I had a few other universities down as well like for example Leicester and Wolverhampton down on my list cause I wouldn't be moving away from home I'd have to travel there. I think I came to Birmingham cause it was good university with a good reputation. (Mahreen Shah, undergraduate, Pakistani, Birmingham)

> The reason why I chose it is because obviously it's a red brick – it's one of the best unis in the North, and because it's got a good reputation, and the reason why I did my PGCE here is because I didn't want to do it elsewhere, I was familiar with Leeds, I liked it, and that's why I wanted to do my course back here. (Rukster Khan, Pakistani graduate, Leeds)

We found a similar pattern of knowledge about the reputation of particular departments or courses at certain universities. In these cases there was evidence of some use of published league tables in order to help them decide which was the best choice for them. This often entailed not just researching institutions but the courses in particular subjects. This was most often the case for those who had successfully applied to university, but was much less common among the sixth-formers who were still thinking about their decisions:

> The Business School is very reputable at Aston University, you get a very good chance of getting a good job after. That's what mostly attracted me, because you get a placement year in between after your second year – Aston Business School is really top in Business Schools, so I thought that I'd get a good job after that – and it has really good links with the placements, and you can get a good job afterwards, straight after your degree like if you do well in your placement year, so I thought that would be the best. (Amina Khanum, Bangladeshi undergraduate, Birmingham)

Because I knew that I wouldn't be able to leave home completely, and go to a far away university and I knew that I'd need to pick a good university like Leeds, like it was suited to my needs because it had a very good reputation for Geography as well. (Saydhah Shah, Indian graduate, Leeds)

Leeds was the highest on the league table for Radiography. One of my teachers at college had been to Leeds University and I had a lot of respect for him. He motivated me and I thought I would follow in his footsteps. And also because Leeds is such a good city, it has good fashion and a really good nightlife. (Saman Kaur, Indian undergraduate, Leeds)

Whilst much of the discussion of league tables tends to focus on those institutions which are highly rated and therefore have positive implications for those who study at them, we found some evidence of the disadvantages that may accrue to those who attend institutions that are low in the hierarchy. In much previous literature it has frequently been recognised that most ethnic minority students attend former polytechnics and that this may lead to later disadvantages (Shiner and Modood, 2002). However, more detailed exploration of this issue has often been lacking.

In particular we have evidence of the young women's own accounts of how some institutions have positive or negative popular stereotypes. This has a number of consequences for those who attend such institutions. Which local university the young woman attended often affected how others in the South Asian community saw them, and those attending these lower status universities were often very aware of the longer term consequences for them. This strong local sense of a hierarchy of local universities seemed to be stronger in the West Midlands rather than in West Yorkshire:

If I had a choice now I don't think I would have gone to UCE, I definitely would have gone to Birmingham. It's a better university and I think it would have given me more optional choices if I'd have gone to Birmingham because no matter what people say, employers do look at your background and they do look at universities and I know if I'd have applied to Birmingham I would have got a place there so that's why. (Ayesha Ali, Bangladeshi graduate, Birmingham)

Well they see UCE as crap basically I suppose they prefer Birmingham or Aston. It's quite weird actually UCE is the only one out that has the LPC, Birmingham don't do it neither does Aston. So I don't see why they can call this university crap when they have this status. (Jaspreet Kaur, UCE graduate, Indian, Birmingham)

Well obviously people think that University of Birmingham are like the higher ranking university out of the three that you've just mentioned and UCE is sort of like the third class university of the three but Wolverhampton is, if you put it in order it would be University of Birmingham, Aston, Wolverhampton and then UCE because when

I started that's how it was but now everything has just changed because the law degree here is more respected now because of the fact that its much more practical and the employers and people see that it's not about theory any more it's about what you learn, the skills that you know so now UCE is just underneath Aston now and Wolverhampton's moved down one notch so ... (Narinder Kaur, Indian graduate, Birmingham)

In the West Midlands, the University of Central England (UCE) in particular was thought by many to have a very negative image. This is not only among the wider South Asian community, but also amongst students in the region. There seemed to be a kind of status competition in the South Asian communities of the West Midlands, where your standing was determined by which local university you attended. This is an interesting translation of established educational hierarchies being imported into status hierarchies among young South Asian people. However, many of those who were attending or had attended UCE were very defensive about its status and reputation:

Within this area everyone says that they think Aston is a good university, my sister went there as well I think it's just because it's quite easy to get into but also it's a good place like a business school and everything and Birmingham is just considered like really really good. I don't know if it's the type of building but also it's like entry requirements are really high, as I said I missed by four marks and they didn't want me there and I think UCE that's considered a sort of dossing place, people do see it as. Actually there are some people though you will say to them which uni do you go to and they will say UCE but they will say it like they are proud of it and other people will say it like oh it's a doss house we mess about all the time so I think it's just what they make of the whole experience really. I did think that Wolverhampton was right at the bottom but there are so many people coming out of it with first class degrees and they are really glad to have gone there so I've realised that the more time you spend at a university then the less conscious you get of where it stands in the league tables and I have got a friend who is always laughing and saying how when she tells people what, they will say to her what are you studying and she says law and then they say where are you studying it and she will say Wolverhampton and the conversation is dead there because she is no longer in competition with anyone. I think actually one of the lecturers admitted that we are on the bottom of the league tables and she was saying you are doing a degree and everything do yourself and favour and try and do well and she was kind of implying that it's bad enough that you got into this university in the first place to study law. (Navjot Kaur, Indian undergraduate, Birmingham)

When I ended up at an ex-polytechnic I had to prove everybody wrong. I had to prove the fact that it wasn't about where I was because I could still prove that I could get the grades or I could hold an intellectual conversation. They might not directly say it but it's the response you get. Say if I went to one person and I said I'm at Cambridge, or if I said I was at UCE, I would get totally different responses. I was part of a society that was an amalgamation of different student forums from three different universities within Birmingham. There was Birmingham which was known as the best university in Birmingham, then you had Aston which was a lower ranking, and then you had UCE which was an ex-polytechnic. I knew people from Birmingham who looked down on us because we were from UCE. If you typecast like that it did have a direct effect on us because then we thought that. (Simra Bhana, Indian graduate Leeds, attended UCE as an undergraduate)

The reputations of universities, be they based on published league tables or popular judgements, not only shape the choices that students make, but also affect how they are seen by others. Unlike previous research (Reay *et al*, 2005) which has asserted that league tables and the reputation of universities did not enter into the calculations of most ethnic minority applicants to university in London, we have found that this does matter for South Asian women in West Yorkshire and especially the West Midlands. Although they may have geographically limited choices of university, they often have a sharp sense of the best local institutions. Sometimes these are grounded in an inspection of the published league tables, but in other instances they are based upon local knowledge, and local judgements about institutional status in the South Asian community. This local knowledge often mirrors the published league tables in relative standing, if not in what they say about different institutions. In this sense, there is no clear division between what has been termed by Reay *et al* (2005) as the cold information of league tables and the hot knowledge of community perspectives.

Young South Asian women were aware of the differences between the two main universities within Leeds, as they were within the West Midlands, although the distinctions did not translate in quite the same way into a community specific status competition. Firstly, within Leeds the women acknowledged the higher status of the University of Leeds to Leeds Metropolitan University. For instance, Aaliyah (a Pakistani undergraduate) went to Leeds University because of its reputation: 'I heard everyone saying it's such a good uni and it's quite well known and everything'. Besides suggestions about the institution in terms of its course, the women went on to distinguish between academic levels of the students at the two universities. Jasmin Ali, another Pakistani student, studies Law at Leeds Metropolitan University and noted the difference between getting a law degree from Leeds Met and from Leeds University: 'in the Met people are not really as clever as people that go to uni.'

The women interviewed at Leeds Metropolitan University had lower expectations of their A level grades, and had therefore applied to former polytechnics as they did not think they were going to get the grades to get in to old universities. This supports the statistical findings that many apply to university with lower A level scores than white students (Taylor, 1993a; Shiner and Modood, 2002). However, others were oblivious to the differences between universities. For instance, Ambran Begum, a Bangladeshi undergraduate, decided to go to Leeds Met and had not even considered Leeds University:

> I don't see a difference, because at the end of the day if I was doing the degree at Leeds uni or even in Huddersfield, it's a degree and I will still get a qualification form it ... so what difference does it make?

In terms of those students currently at university, there was huge significance placed on the prestige of a university in the vast majority of instances. All the women at Leeds University, for example, said that they had applied there because of its reputation of being a good university. This was the case even with those who were living at home with their parents. The women who studied at the Metropolitan University acknowledged the difference between the two institutions. They also acknowledged the differences in job prospects; they perceived employers as being more interested in students who had attended old universities such as Leeds. Despite this widespread knowledge of the varying prestige of institutions, we did not encounter many young women who had applied to Oxford or Cambridge. For the most part they felt that those universities were totally out of their league.

A suitable course?

A factor often mentioned in accounts of middle-class choice of university is the depth of research that they carry out into finding the right kind of degree and institution (Reay *et al*, 2005). For these students and their parents it is the perceived quality of the university and the suitability of the course that determines choice of location. We found something like this among many of the young women, although, it was not clearly related to class background. It appeared that a significant minority looked in more detail at the course and the institution, and this was often a more significant factor than location in their choice of institution. These young women, however, did not make explicit reference to league tables, so their criteria are rather different from those who did rely upon league tables upon which to base their decisions.

For example, Farrah Mughal, a Pakistani graduate in the West Midlands, had secured a place at Birmingham University, yet she chose to attend the lower status University of Wolverhampton. She explained this in terms of the nature of the course, as she saw the course at Birmingham as 'too theoretical', whilst that at Wolverhampton she felt suited her better due to its practical orientation. In this instance, a vocational degree with its assumptions of creating more employable graduates was seen as more suitable than the academic and high status theory-based degree at a red brick university:

> I got a place at Birmingham University but which I declined that was all theory based but I wanted to do something that was more practical and Wolverhampton was a good campus to do theory and practical. And I came out with a 2.1.

This theme of choosing an appropriate course within geographical limits was something that appeared in the narratives of several of the Bangladeshi and Pakistani women. This focus on the availability of a particular course contrasts with the findings of others such as Reay *et al* (2005), who stress the way in which ethnic minority students in general rely on hot community knowledge or advice from friends and relatives. It is all the more striking, given that many of those who talked about the significance of the course were Pakistani and Bangladeshi women from working-class backgrounds, with little previous family experience of going to university:

> Initially I wanted to do a combination degree which was half Computing and half Law which I did do one year of, but then I found that my heart wasn't really in the computing and so I switched. Wolverhampton was the only university that was local enough that did the combination which was initially why I chose it. (Iman Karim, Pakistani undergraduate, Birmingham)

> Because Leeds University didn't have the youth and community studies course I don't think they do that. I don't know I just opted for Leeds Met because it was on. I don't know why I didn't go to Leeds Uni I just opened up a prospectus and there was youth and community studies so I thought well that's the course that I want to do I might as well do it so I didn't even bother looking into any other colleges or any other universities ... I just thought Leeds Met because you know both Huddersfield and Wakefield they were both doing it but the title was slightly different, so I went on the website and I just looked up what the course entailed and what they were offering and what kind of modules that would be of interest to me and the ones at Leeds Met they were more interesting to me and they were closer to home so I just went for that. (Jabeen Ahmad, Bangladeshi undergraduate, Leeds)

> The course really. With English you get a lot of traditional English courses like Chaucer and Shakespeare which I love but I wanted something more, I wanted some linguistics. I wanted a flexible course where I could include some Sociology. I didn't just want to trap myself into English and then think what am I going to do. I was always interested in Sociology and Social Policy. But I really wanted to go to

Nottingham and I didn't get in. I don't know why. My predicted grades were higher than what they wanted but I just didn't get in. (SimiBanu, Indian undergraduate, Leeds)

The ethnic mix of institutions

Finally, there is the issue of the perceived ethnic composition of the university, and the role that this may play in a student's choice of university. Reay *et al* (2005) have suggested that the perceived ethnic mix of a university is an important factor influencing the decisions of young ethnic minority people about which universities to apply for. It is suggested that ethnic minority students tend to choose those institutions that are perceived to have a significant proportion of ethnic minority undergraduates. In contrast to that generalisation from a much more ethnically mixed sample in London, we found little evidence that this was an important factor among South Asian women in the West Midlands and West Yorkshire. It did appear to influence a minority of the young women, but in rather different ways from those suggested by Reay *et al*.

Firstly, there were those who avoided institutions with a perceived large number of South Asian students. For a minority of either students or parents, these were seen as undesirable places to attend. A few young women wanted to get away from places where they were known. For example, Jameela Yaqoob came from Rossendale to study in Leeds in preference to Manchester:

Because I didn't really want to go to Manchester because I knew loads of people going to Manchester and so I wanted something different – so the next option was coming to Leeds, which was quite similar to Manchester in the sense that it's quite multi-cultural and there are a lot of things going on. So, I came to Leeds – and I came to the Open Day and it was really nice. (Jameela Yaqoob, Bangladeshi, Leeds undergraduate)

Secondly, a few of the young women reported that, for their parents, some universities with a perceived large percentage of South Asian students were seen as morally undesirable places. They were perceived as places where the young women could meet South Asian men in an un-chaperoned environment. Alternatively, such universities might be seen as not having a high standing in the community or in league tables, a point which harks back to our earlier discussion of the perceived standing of different universities in each region:

I think my parents did not want me to go to Bradford from what they had heard about it. Just the fact that there are a lot of Asians there, and they were not too keen on that idea. So my dad really didn't want me to go there. They wanted me to go to

Leeds either Leeds Met or Leeds Uni he wasn't bothered about that. But after a lot of perseverance he agreed to Bradford. But they don't regret me going there. Once I got settled into my course they were ok about it. (Adiba Kamran, Pakistani graduate, Leeds)

Like I've been there a couple times before and it seems like a fun place to be. I thought I could study here and no other local university had my course and for this course it's got a good reputation. UCE did as well but my parents didn't want me to go to UCE because you know it's got quite a bad reputation. They didn't really want me to go to Wolverhampton and then there was nowhere else and I didn't move out so. (Beenish Kaur, Indian undergraduate, Birmingham)

Thirdly, a further area of concern about the ethnic composition of universities expressed by a few of the young women was in terms of moving away to a largely white environment. This raises issues that we pursue in more detail in a later chapter concerned with racism and Islamophobia. This was expressed in terms of the ways in which the social life of overwhelmingly white universities is geared towards forms of leisure that were seen as incompatible with being a Muslim. This was seen as resulting in the isolation of South Asian Muslim women at university when they move away from home:

It's very difficult I mean, I wanted to, to begin with I wanted to however looking at it in retrospect I'm glad I never did, a lot of people that I know, a lot of Asian girls that I know find it very difficult integrating into, because when you move away you don't know anyone you know nobody, the only way you get to know people is by doing what they do around you so everybody else is going out, going out clubbing or something that the student life revolves around it's not something being an Asian Muslim. On top of that it's not something we do and that makes it difficult and you feel the loneliness then. (Bushra Kauser, Pakistani undergraduate, Birmingham)

However, when we asked about whether or not the young women had ever thought about applying to the most elite universities – Oxford and Cambridge – their perceptions of the ethnic composition of these institutions came to the fore. It was only in relation to these universities that we found anything like the views discussed by Reay *et al* (2005), where ethnic minority applicants tend not to apply to universities that have a reputation for being overwhelmingly white. Mostly, the young women replied that Oxford and Cambridge were entirely unrealistic for them, given their A level grades, or they regarded the places as being for the upper classes. The change to a language and imagery of class here is also significant. As Salima Azar, a Pakistani sixth-former, said when asked whether she would apply to Oxford or Cambridge like her cousin: 'No cos they're all up their arses!' Nevertheless it was striking how the theme of the whiteness of Oxford and Cambridge was seen by the young women as a factor excluding them. Often this was from women who had been encouraged to apply to Oxford and Cambridge or knew relatives and friends who had applied, were attending or had attended one these universities. Much of the time it seems that these perceptions were based on their own experiences or those of people they knew:

> Well my parents actually did ask me to apply to Cambridge because the rate I was going I was going to get better grades than I actually did get. Oxford I just did not like the look of completely didn't – that looked like the most stuck up place in the whole wide world. Cambridge looked kind of alright but I just it was just the fact of not having any Asians there which really is quite a put off. (Bushra Kauser, Pakistani undergraduate, Birmingham)

> My cousin's actually applied there she got all As, she went there visited it and got offered a place but she turned it down. After visiting it she wasn't really comfortable there, because there are not many Asian people there. Because if you have been brought up in a those kinds of school where you have majority Asian people it is then more comfortable. (Sukwinder Kaur, Indian undergraduate, Birmingham)

> I'm drawn to very cosmopolitan areas where there is a mixture of religion and culture, and I thought to myself I could go there and there would be a very strong white culture and I would be like you know when you're on the peripheral and the engagement with you isn't that great. A bit superficial and so on, I was thinking I don't want to be that, so that would have been a wrong decision for me. (Fatima Begum, Bangladeshi undergraduate, Leeds)

> No. I didn't think I would achieve the grades. And secondly it was fitting in that kind of an environment cause they are well known for its middle-class white students. And coming from a minority myself I would have felt really displaced. (Tahira Safder, Pakistani graduate, Leeds)

Recent research on why students do not apply to Cambridge has suggested that fear of failure, worries about application process and the hard work involved discouraged applicants (Whitehead *et al*, 2006). However, that quantitative study did not specifically ask about ethnicity, or perceptions of the university. Whereas our findings are specific to South Asian women, but they do show that the perceived whiteness and upper class character of Oxford and Cambridge discourages applicants from this group. In this way, the whiteness and élite character of Oxford and Cambridge might be reproduced as a self-fulfilling prophecy.

Conclusion

The evidence and arguments in this chapter challenge established thinking about South Asian women and choice in higher education in a number of ways. They also present a challenge for some of the recent theorising in this area, especially that derived from the thinking of Bourdieu.

Firstly, there is no singular South Asian social capital, cultural capital or habitus that is being expressed through the actions, choices and decisions in relation to higher education among South Asian women, as has been suggested by some recent authors (Abbas, 2004; Modood, 2004). Secondly, such theorising glosses over the real contests that go on between parents and children over subject choice in particular. Thirdly, as a consequence they are unable to account for either the patterns of university application, or subject choice, or the changes in those patterns. We think that the evidence presented in this chapter highlights the limitations of the essentialist thinking and failure to examine the interactions involved in making decisions about higher education amongst those writers influenced by cultural capital and social capital theory.

We have examined how the young women decided to go to university, whilst attempting to recognise that these decisions are complex processes, sometimes involving difficult negotiations with parents and other relatives. This has entailed looking at some of the influences on their decisions about going to university in the first place, and then the young women's choice of qualifications, subjects and university.

We found that early parental support and expectations were crucial for the decision to apply to university among all South Asian ethnic groups. For the young Bangladeshi and Pakistani women, this support was instrumental in their eyes, in that they told us how their parents saw higher education largely in terms of future earning potential. In addition, Indian women often reported that there was strong school support for their desire to go to university. For a large minority of students, changes in their lifestyle and independence were also important reasons for going to university, and role models were important for most of the women interviewed.

Another important sphere of parental influence was over subjects to study at A level and at university. Parents often influenced the choice of A levels and degree subjects, showing a strong preference for qualifications leading to careers in the traditional professions such as Law or Medicine, even when their daughters were relatively weak in these academic fields. For many of the young women, there were quite distinct hierarchies of local universities, and these tended to mirror published league tables. Furthermore, many of the young women who were at university had made use of league tables when choosing their courses. The ethnic mix of a university did not seem to be important in their choice of institution, as reported for some ethnic minority students in other studies (Reay *et al*, 2005). However, many of the academic high achievers did not choose Oxford or Cambridge due their perceived middle-class character and, especially, their overwhelmingly white culture.

5

Negotiating University: plans for marriage and studying at home

Whether or not many young South Asian women get to university is shaped by how far they are able to negotiate with their parents two important issues: marriage and leaving home. In this chapter we examine these issues and the patterns that emerge from our analysis, especially with respect to ethnicity and religion. The questions of marriage and leaving home are inter-related, as it is often assumed in some South Asian communities that a young woman will not leave home until she is married.

Contemporary images of South Asian women continue to be embodied within cultural and religious frameworks and consequently they are often presented as essentialised and oppressed figures of victim-hood and despair (Ahmad, 2003; Shain, 2003). One way in which this is so is through assumptions about the practices of marriage. Within our analysis of marriage and young South Asian women, we have found the opposite of this stereotype. Generally, we have found that women negotiate with their parents between their own expectations and choices and their parents' preferences. However, the terms and dynamics of this negotiation vary between ethnic groups, religious beliefs and social class backgrounds.

Within South Asian communities, there has been evidence that the attitudes of young South Asians on arranged marriages are shifting from those of their parents (Stopes-Roe and Cochrane, 1990; Anwar, 1998). This has been found to be more the case among Sikhs and Hindus than among South Asian Muslims (Modood *et al*, 1997). For the Sikh and Hindu young women, we found that their experiences were in keeping with these findings, as they failed to see marriage in terms of their parents' and their own decision, their choice was a mixture of both. Furthermore, even though the individuals were making their own decisions, parents were closely involved.

However, it is among Muslim women where we note significant changes between the generations; for the Muslim women of Pakistani, Bangladeshi and Indian heritage, it was clear that changes were moving in the same direction as the Hindus and Sikhs and to some extent influencing their behaviour. Any generalisations about Muslims must therefore take into account the variations of experiences within each of these groups (Ballard, 1994).

Within the Bangladeshi community, as among many South Asian communities, marriage connections have previously worked to maintain and strengthen links between kin in Bangladeshi and, more recently, it has provided opportunities for Bengalis to strengthen ties with British resident kin by marrying in Britain (Gardner and Shukur, 1994). The Bangladeshi community within Britain is of relatively recent origin, largely made up of people who have come from the rural area of Sylhet and have settled within established Bengali communities. It is a close-knit community which holds on to the traditional values of Bangladesh, including those related to marriage. Arranged marriages are seen to be preferred within this community, whereby the parents and possibly some other family elders play a role in the selection of a partner and in arranging the marriage.

There are a number of sources of variation in relation to marriage and leaving home to go to university. These include ethnicity, religion and class background. As we interviewed young women before, during and after going to university, we are also able to compare the views of women at these three different stages of their educational careers.

Very few of the women in our study were married, however, our interviews included questions on how the young women thought that their marriage would take place. Those we interviewed described the role they expected of their parents in the choice of their spouse. Furthermore, in discussions about marriage in the interviews, it became clear that, although many of the young women talked about arranged marriage, significant modifications have been made to what the practice is often thought to be.

In the case of some of those studying A levels, their decisions about education were seen as dictated by their impending marriage. This is an issue that previous research has highlighted as being specific to South Asian women, especially those from Muslim backgrounds (Ahmad *et al*, 2003). In some instances these women were aware their marriages were being arranged by their parents. Their decisions on whether or not to pursue higher education, and in what locality, were bound up with decisions about their marriage. As some of the young women talked about choosing which higher education institutions they could apply to, it became clear how limited their control could be over this aspect of their lives.

Some of them, especially the Bangladeshi and Pakistani women in the sixth forms, described how they may have to pull out of their education at any time. They talked about a relationship with their parents that was quite different from that described by most of the Indian women and indeed some of the other Bangladeshi and Pakistani women. Whilst the majority of parents placed a major importance on education, there were others who were the complete opposite; their daughters were allowed to study but it was seen as less of a serious educational strategy and future career-building activity than as a time-filling experience until they found eligible men to marry. Consequently, their daughters were unable to make firm decisions on their future with respect to education.

The Bangladeshi women

Marriage was a central issue for all of the Bangladeshi young women. For the unmarried Bangladeshis studying either at A level or degree level, their plans for their education were sometimes dictated by their impending marriage. They told us that their parents were keen for them to be married as soon as possible. The young women described the role of their parents in the choice of their spouses, and how they would be consulted and have a say in the choice. Jameela Yaqoob, currently at university, talked about the negotiation process which she expects will take place:

> I wouldn't just bring someone home and say 'look, I've found a guy for myself and I'm going to get married to him'. I'm not going to do it like that . His family gets involved, and then it's going to be more like an arranged process going on rather than me getting him and saying 'I've found a guy, I'm going to get married to him'. If they say 'no' then I'd put my foot down and say 'I want to marry him!'

For the young women themselves, this kind of development of a negotiated marriage was viewed in a positive and progressive light in comparison to past ways in which their parents or older sisters had been married. The young women viewed these changes as examples of parents accommodating their children's changing preferences. They made reference to the types of marriages which older people in their community had undergone, and talked about the new freedoms they were experiencing. Nevertheless, many young Bangladeshi women often referred to the fact they were having arranged marriages, and some were aware their marriages were being arranged by their parents during their studies. Their decision on whether or not to pursue higher education depended on the speed at which their parents would find suitable partners. According to Alpha Rehman, a Bangladeshi sixth-former:

> I am hoping they find someone after my studies, cos then I can just concentrate on my studies, it they find someone in the middle of my education then it will probably ruin it.

The young women were asked why parents felt it necessary for them to marry so young. Often this was because it was felt that it was more difficult for an educated woman to find a partner. According to Amina Chaudhury, who re-fused to get married before completing her degree, her parents are currently looking for a husband for her. However, this is proving difficult, as she argues that having an educated daughter-in-law is perceived as a threat by some in her community: 'A lot of people are daunted by the experience of women having a degree because they are a lot more articulate.'

We also encountered some young women who had come out of the education system to get married, but then returned. Zoreena Bibi, a Bangladeshi graduate, went to Bangladesh at the age of 16 and was married. However, later on she went back into education as a part-time student. 'I felt I was missing something and I realised that education is so important you can't go any-where without education and I always dreamt of doing a degree'. However, we encountered very few instances of this route into higher education, as most of the young women were deferring their marriages until after they had graduated. This was not unusual; quite a few of the Bangladeshi women chose education as a solution to the inevitability of marriage.

For many of the Bangladeshi women, negotiated marriage was a very recent development in their communities, and it was centrally related to their plans and decisions about going to university. The opportunity to go to university was used to defer and negotiate the timing of marriage.

The Indian women
For the young women of Indian descent, their discussion of arranged mar-riage involved far more negotiation with their parents, although love mar-riages were also favoured within these groups and, to some extent, allowed by parents. In many of the households, the Indian young women were able to define the type of marriage they wanted, and they were the final arbiters in the choice of their marriage partner. Marriage was seen as less important and less stressful in comparison to the Muslim young women. For the Indian

young women in general, parents avoided the subject of marriage until their daughter finished their degrees and, even then, the young women negotiated more time with their parents to allow them to start their careers. For example, according to Saman Kaur, a Sikh undergraduate:

> They know that after university I will be going home. They have mentioned to me in a few months they will start looking and I have told them no as I don't want to get married for a least a couple of years yet. I want to get settled in my career, progress to where I want to be, be satisfied with who I am and then get married I think ... they don't have much choice in the matter really.

The Indian young women had more control over their marriage plans and their future. They told their parents when and if they would marry, and what type of marriage they were having. The emphasis was not on their parents' preferences, but on the daughters themselves who, in some instances, resorted to threats to make sure their wishes were respected. Davinder Kaur, for example says: 'They knew I'm not ready for it so why would they talk to me about it? I said if they tried to push it on me I would leave home.'

When the daughters did consent to their parents finding someone for them to marry, parents would invite prospective husbands to the home so that their daughter could view him and then decide if she wanted to pursue the relationship. This meant further viewing sessions, the more liberal parents permitted their daughters to meet the man socially before deciding whether or not to become engaged. It was also imperative for most of the Indian families that the groom match the caste of the bride. Leena Mistry, a Hindu undergraduate, explained her dilemma, where her mother objected to her wish to marry her higher caste boyfriend. The caste of her boyfriend was seen by her mother both as a source of personal incompatibility, and a reason for gossip in the community:

> Yeah I've been with him for three years now but she doesn't want me to marry him but I think it's because she's worried about me. I think because if you get married out of caste because every caste does things differently and she's not sure how well I would fit in to somebody else's caste and she thinks I'd struggle and because other people would start talking that she's married out of caste and things.

Whilst highly formalised patterns of arranged marriage are seemingly in decline amongst communities of Indian origin, there are still community spaces and events where it is seen as appropriate for young people to mix and make contact with each other. According to Pooja Parmar, an Indian graduate, weddings were a prime place for getting the phone numbers of eligible men. She goes on to describe how this can then lead to an introduction to the parents, or the parents of the two young people would make contact between themselves on hearing of the contact between the couple:

> If you like someone and someone likes you we could probably speak to them. We'd probably exchange numbers and I'd speak to them for a bit, if I like them I would introduce him to my parents and then take things from there ... or if the guy says he likes the girl then his parents will probably find out whose daughter it is and approach them and ask if it's okay if they exchange numbers.

For the Indian young women, their parents had often had a wider variety of marriage compared to the other groups. The parents were less likely to have had an arranged marriage themselves than the parents of the Bangladeshi and Pakistani young women. This meant that it was not an issue for some of the young women although arranged marriages were still preferred among many families. Consequently, there was far more flexibility for the Hindu and Sikh respondents than for those of the other groups we interviewed. Nevertheless, there was still a preference for arranged marriage in some Indian families. According to Kiran Kaur, a Sikh sixth-former, for example:

> I've told my parents that am not having an arranged marriage. I think they're ok with that but they still see that as the right way. Well my parents didn't really have an arranged marriage themselves, they knew each other from before as well. And my aunt didn't have an arranged marriage at all, so I think they will be ok with me having a love marriage.

What is also significant in this area is that higher levels of parental involvement in the choice of a partner were more likely with the parents who had fewer or no qualifications. For example, both Kamaljeet Kaur's parents are manual workers; her mother works in a packing factory and her father is a truck driver. Their perception of marriage differed from that of their daughter. Kamaljeet talked about the restrictions she has had on her life with respect to partnerships. Her parents refused her the degree of choice that other Hindu parents had given their daughters. She explains why, as follows:

> My cousins have done a lot of things that she [her mother] didn't really accept ... my dad's brother's daughters ran away one actually got married to a guy from a different religion and the other one was pregnant when she was 16. My mum sees all that and just clamped down and restrained me from any sort of activity to stop myself from getting into a situation like that she didn't want me to go into a university away from home.

Kamaljeet was engaged and due to marry the following year. She describes the process of this engagement which she called 'very, very traditional' in the following way:

> We were introduced once and we spoke to each other for a couple of hours and we sort of had to make a decision from there. It sounds really harsh but that's sort of the way it works.

For some of the Indian women, marriage was seen as inevitable, and the option was marriage or university. For Jeevan Mudan, an Indian graduate in Leeds, one of the reasons that she went to university was as a way of delaying marriage. As she told us: 'I thought it was a way of putting off things which I thought was going to be inevitable like marriage off a bit longer that's all.'

The Pakistani women

The Pakistani community continues to be seen as conservative in terms of its marriage patterns (Modood *et al*, 1997: 317-8). Whilst changes are occurring within the Bangladeshi and Indian communities, within the Pakistani sample there seemed to be the most evidence of changes of opinion and practice taking place between generations. Within this category, the individuals reveal traditional arranged marriages to be in decline. Instead, consultation and negotiation now take place between the parents and their child. The young women saw this shift as a new freedom in comparison to past restrictions.

In this context, Farzana Amin's marriage was most unusual in being what she described as traditional and conservative. Farzana, a sixth-form student studying for a BTEC and planning to go to university, told us about being engaged to a cousin – the son of her mother's sister and father's brother – at the age of three. She rebelled against this arranged marriage, but she was still married to the young man in Pakistan, having negotiated her path into education with her parents. As she explained to us:

> It was arranged since I was 3 years old. Ever since I've been growing up everybody's been saying it oh you're going to get married to him and when the time came I said I wasn't going to go but my parents said yes you are going to, you can come back and go to college you can go to university you can do what you want so I thought fine, I went saw him didn't like him, got married anyway.

We asked Farzana why she had married him if she didn't like him. She explained the dense network of kin relationships that surrounded the arrangement. Consequently there were obligations that she felt towards her parents, and the fear that they would lose face amongst their closest relatives in Pakistan. Together these made it difficult for her simply to reject the marriage: 'Because it'd be embarrassing for my parents if I went all the way there and said no ... it was my dad's brother's son and my mum's sister's son so it was like my brother.'

Having failed to consummate the relationship, Farzana's aim on arriving back in the UK was to have his proposal to come to the UK rejected. Such early engagements and arrangements of marriage are the exception, and often meet with resistance from one or both partners. Despite such instances giving arranged marriages an overwhelmingly negative image, some of the Pakistani young women told us that they preferred to have an arranged marriage. For example, Mehwish Begum, a student at a further education college, was opting for an arranged marriage. She favoured this on the grounds that she wanted the same kind of marriage as her older siblings which, in her view, had been successful arranged marriages: 'I've seen my brothers' and sisters' marriages and they have worked out really good as well and I trust my parents to find someone good for me.'

There were other young women who wanted to have arranged marriages, but stressed the way in which they would be negotiated. In the majority of cases, the young women had a veritable shopping list of what they were looking for in a husband. These were extensively discussed with parents and siblings, and, according to the young women, parents were very keen to take full account of their daughters' preferences. For example, Shameem Khan, a Pakistani undergraduate, told us that:

> I would say more arranged, but with slight agreement on both halves so it isn't forced ... The thing is they are not actively looking. And when they are they are not going to look for somebody who has got a degree, firstly I have told them I want somebody who is good with their religion, personally that is my first option. Education I'm not too bothered about as long as he is a good guy, family orientated and hard working; they know what I'm like, they know I don't like lazy people and I'm not too keen on big families so my dad says I'll find you an orphan!

There was also a definite class difference among the Pakistani sample in relation to views about marriage. This is contrary to the findings from a national survey in the 1990s (Modood *et al*, 1997: 317-8). Those from a higher-class background would point out the differences between their families who were educated and in professional jobs in comparison to families who were less educated and in manual jobs. Jasmin Ali, an undergraduate law student, is from a middle-class background, her parents are both educated and in professional jobs. When we interviewed her, she was studying at university and she talked about her relationship with her boyfriend who is from a traditional Pakistani household, and a working-class background. Her family would not object to her boyfriend, providing he was Muslim, but she talked about how she faces abuse from his sisters. She talked about the complications they would have in their marriage: 'They just are too strict in their family background upbringing and everything, they really are strict.'

When asked what type of marriage they would like, most of the Pakistani young women talked about a negotiated marriage. This was the most typical kind of view that we found among the Pakistani women. Within this category of negotiated marriage, there are a variety of routes that the women have in mind. Parents could find the partners, or the women could find a partner for approval by the parents. According to Shazia Manzoor, an undergraduate student, she wants what she calls a negotiated marriage because:

> If I had a love marriage and my parents objected to it then I don't think I would be entirely happy about it. So if I did fall in love with somebody I would like my parents to agree to it as well. And if they found someone then I would like to know the person meet him and then decide.

What was interesting was that, although marriage was something that was seen as inevitable by the young women, they were adamant about pursuing their education, irrespective of getting married. For example, according to Farhana Sheikh, a sixth-former:

> Even if I was going to get you know married in the next three years, I'm still thinking of carrying on with what I'm wanting to do, not just to stop because you are married or whatever. It's one of things to carry on and seek your knowledge.

There were some cases when students were already married and were pursuing their education after marriage. In many instances this was the contract that was made before marriage between her parents and her husband's family. There were a number of reasons given for this. For instance, according to Rafika Amin, a Pakistani in a Leeds sixth form, who is married and now living with her in-laws' family, these concerned the moral risks of going to university: 'At uni you get led on by people ... you do stupid things ... I want to know when I go home at the end of the day I have somebody at home waiting for me.'

Parental choice of marriage partners was found among all groups to some extent, but was more likely among those with fewer or no qualifications as found in previous national surveys (Modood *et al*, 1997). With our Bangladeshi sample, it was evenly spread across the social classes, however, with the Pakistanis and Indians it was found more in the lower than the higher occupational classes. Almost all the young women from each of the ethnic groups wished to choose their own husbands, but many were resigned to varying degrees of arranged or negotiated marriage. The localities where we interviewed, Leeds and Birmingham, are in regions that have been documented as having higher levels of parentally arranged marriage during the 1990s. Both these regions, the West Midlands and Yorkshire, had the highest proportion of South Asians who had had their parents choose their spouse (Modood *et al*, 1997: 317-18).

We found that marriage was one of the central life plans of the young women we interviewed that was related to decisions about education in quite specific ways that are quite unlike the majority white population. For most of the Indian students, marriage planning was not such a central concern, although a number did tell us that going to university or getting married were the options that they felt they faced as teenagers. For many of the Bangladeshi and Pakistani women, decisions around marriage and negotiations with their parents about this were more central. A minority had married before going to university. Some of the young women in the sixth form especially saw marriage as a risk that could disrupt their education at any point. However, most had deferred their marriage until they had completed their degrees.

Leaving home or living at home?

Studying at university for South Asian women involves a critical decision not only about which university to attend and which course to study, but also about whether or not to stay at home with their parents or move away to study. In the more general literature on university choice, this is treated as a class-based issue. It is assumed that those from working-class backgrounds have either limited economic resources, limited knowledge about their choices or choose the local university as it suits people like themselves (Reay *et al*, 2005: 86-96). Consequently, they remain living in the parental home whilst studying at university. Connor *et al* (2004: 54) noted that some South Asian Muslim female students might encounter parental preferences for them to remain at home whilst attending university. In other studies of South Asian women and higher education, this issue is often mentioned, but not considered in any detail (eg Dale *et al*, 2002). However, we have found it to be one of the most important factors differentiating Muslim from Non-Muslim women. In the following sections, we consider the different responses to this issue and examine some of the influences on the decisions that they were making.

Non-Muslim Indian women

All the non-Muslim Indian students currently at university appeared to have had the option of leaving home. These women did acknowledge the reservations of their families, in particular their parents, about them leaving home. Although the parents had reservations, it was not such a big issue as it was for the Muslim women of Bangladeshi or Pakistani origin. The parents of the non-Muslim Indian women did not prevent them from moving away to university despite their concern. According to Kalpana Bharati, a Hindu currently at university:

> My parents didn't want me to come to Leeds because they thought it was a bit far
> ... but I thought it was just right because it's only about seventy miles to Nottingham,
> two hours on the coach and an hour's drive.

Leaving home has undeniably brought about changes in the identity of those young women who did so. In particular, a sense of independence was frequently commented upon. Isha Sharma, an Indian student currently at university, discussed this in more detail:

> I enjoy the independence so much. I had a lot of independence at home and it is
> very different living by yourself. It makes you grow up a lot. You have to fend for
> yourself ...

A factor often mentioned in accounts of middle-class choice of university is the depth of research that parents and offspring carry out into finding the right kind of degree and institution (Reay *et al*, 2005). For the middle-classes, it is the perceived quality of the university and the suitability of the course that determines choice of location. We found something like this among many of the Indian non-Muslim women that we interviewed, and this does perhaps reflect the more middle-class and highly educated background of some of the Indian women's parents. It appeared that they looked in more detail at the course and the institution, and this was often a more significant factor than location in their choice of institution.

Leena Mistry, for example, talked about her psychology degree at Leeds and compared it to Cardiff, which she regarded as a better course, and said she regretted not investigating the course further before starting. Nina Patel told us that she also chose the best universities for the course she wanted to do when she applied through UCAS. Her driving factor was not locality but the course itself: 'Leeds is the best uni in the north, I like it here it's very multi-cultural here.'

Unlike the Muslim women, many of the non-Muslim Indian women who chose a local university more often did so for reasons of convenience, and sometimes they chose a local university in preference to a place that they had secured at a higher-status institution. This has clear echoes of the working-class patterns of choice of local institutions described by Reay *et al* (2005). As several Indian students told us:

> It's closer to home. I did apply for Birmingham and I did get accepted but then I thought to myself it's all the travelling, coming, going and I didn't want the head-ache. Birmingham Uni from my house is about an hour and a half and Wolver-hampton's fifteen minutes ... my dad drops me off. That's another thing I save money (laughs) because dad drops me off I don't have to travel. (Mandeep Kaur, Indian undergraduate, Birmingham)

> I thought of Birmingham but travelling every single day I thought I couldn't be bothered to do that. Wolverhampton is the easiest place to get to and plus my parents don't want to waste money on travelling like the loan they want me to save it. (Kushwant Kaur, Indian undergraduate, Birmingham)

Most of those who had graduated reflected back at length on the decisions about leaving home or staying at home to study and the consequences of this. These women are worth considering separately, as we are able to examine some of the consequences of the restricted geographical choice that some of them faced. This confirmed the difference between the ethnicities and religious groups that we had found among the current undergraduates. The non-Muslim Indian women who had graduated had generally had a wider choice of institutions than the Bangladeshi or Pakistani women. Pooja Parmar, an Indian graduate, whose parents would not have minded if she had left home, told us: 'I could go anywhere I wanted to or where my degree took me to. It was my choice'.

The Muslim women

For the Muslim women, leaving home to study away was a major issue. Often this would involve considerable negotiation with their parents, and those who did move away from the family home to study sometimes faced considerable obstacles persuading their parents to agree. The following examples illustrate a variety of general aspects of geographical boundedness of some of the young women's choice of university. In some instances, wider family, such as brothers, were also influential, even specifying particular institutions based upon their perceptions of those universities' suitability for their sisters. Offers of places on what the women saw as more suitable courses were in some cases turned down in favour of an institution that they could attend whilst living at home with their parents:

> I had the option from Huddersfield, Bradford and Leeds and my parents and my older brother they don't like the Huddersfield culture the students there and in Bradford and Leeds Met so they were like 'the only university you're going to you

can't stay away it has to be Leeds Uni, Huddersfield and Bradford too many Asian people there you get mixed in with the wrong crowd' and everything and they don't like that they actually limited it down for me 'that's the only place you're going to'. (Azra Munir, Pakistani undergraduate, Leeds)

To be honest with you initially I wanted to go to Aston University in Birmingham I always wanted to do Law and they offered a course legal executive management and it sounded really good I researched into it a bit. I got my grades worked hard for them but my parents were quite reluctant to let me go to Aston University so then Bradford was my insurance choice business management that was something I wasn't thinking about I did it at A-levels and I wasn't keen on it but at that moment in time I think I was pressurised into either stay local or not go at all so I went to Bradford and did business management. (Saima Mamood, Pakistani graduate, Leeds)

I applied to loads of universities within Leeds because my parents weren't wanting me to go away from home so I applied at Leeds Met, Leeds University, Bradford, Huddersfield, Sheffield and that's about it really. I applied at Manchester as well got a place at Manchester but my parents weren't happy about me going away. I didn't get a place at Leeds University I got my place here which is the closest to home. (Kamaljeet Kaur, Indian graduate, Leeds)

According to Sadia Hussain, a Pakistani Muslim: 'there is stuff going on at home and you get away from all that stuff. It's like a fresh start'. But she failed to convince her parents to let her move away to go to university. Similar sentiments were expressed by some of the Muslim women who encountered problems in convincing their mothers and fathers to allow them to leave home to study, given what the rest of the community would think. Thus the opposition comes not only from parents, but is partly due to the parents' fear of disapproval or loss of face among the local community:

Like I said that I wanted to stay at home moving away wasn't an option. If I did move it would have been a taboo kind of factor ... especially for a girl, and the community in which I live in I don't know any girl who has moved away for uni. It's seen as that parents are no longer responsible for their daughters, and it's not seen very Islamic as well. (Miriam Patel, Indian Muslim, Leeds)

... it was a bit strange cos I did geography and sociology but I didn't apply for geography at first. I only applied for sociology and psychology so I applied at Leeds, Leeds Met, Huddersfield, Bradford I applied for close ones near by cos I knew that I wouldn't be able to live at university I'd rather commute from home ... because I'm a Muslim my parents weren't too happy with me living by myself and I wouldn't feel comfortable living by myself so I think it's easier for me as a Muslim to stay at home and commute in and out and my parents helped me out as well I wouldn't be that much independent to live away. (Priya Chupra, Indian Muslim sixth-former, Leeds)

However, moving away from home also brought advantages for some of the young women that we interviewed. In general we found that the young women who were at university or who had graduated did not regret their choice of university, or their decision to either stay at home or leave home.

For some of the young Muslim women that we interviewed, leaving home was not particularly important and did not involve conflict or negotiation with parents. For example, Jabeen Ahmad could not see the logic of moving away from home for the sake of it: 'If I can get an education right on my doorstep why am I going to travel all the way to wherever?' Consequently, she applied only to local universities.

More women of Bangladeshi heritage were studying away from home than their Pakistani counterparts, and there was a difference within the Indian category between the Muslim and non-Muslim women. The Muslim women from an Indian background, like the Bangladeshi and Pakistani young women, for the most part applied to and attended local universities, whereas almost all the Hindu and Sikh women studied away from home as undergraduates. There were several reasons for this. Some of the Muslim women had the choice to leave home, such as Shameem, a Pakistani undergraduate, who applied to local universities. She reported that:

> I applied to Sheffield, Sheffield Hallam, Leeds and loads of others and I told my dad if he was fine with me going out and about and he said yes he was. But one thing was I got rejected from Sheffield so that was out of the question and then the comparison was between Sheffield Hallam and Leeds and Leeds was my option. I wanted to stay at home to be honest; I didn't want to go out.

Shazia, another Pakistani undergraduate, also decided to stay living at home with her parents for her university studies: 'I wanted to be close to home get home safely and quickly'. She says her parents didn't say anything about this issue: 'my parents wouldn't have objected to it, but I didn't want to move myself'.

In these instances, where the young women automatically chose a local institution without even thinking about moving away, their situation is perhaps closest to that found among working-class students in other studies (Reay *et al*, 2005). However, in general the reasons for Muslim women studying near to their home were quite different from the reasons of finance or convenience, or attendance at a university that traditionally recruits students from a working-class background that were suggested in Reay *et al*'s study. For our Muslim students, the main reasons were the preferences of parents and the views of the wider community.

100

For most of the Pakistani women, leaving home to study was problematic. When probed about the reasons why, they often talked about their religion being an important factor in this. Quite often they were already aware of what the community expectations were, as other slightly older women had studied at university and stayed at home with their parents. For instance, Rahila Akhtar, an Indian Muslim graduate, told us she knew her parents would not allow her to leave home to study at university:

> I applied to Leeds, Leeds Met, Huddersfield, and Bradford. I applied to the close ones near by cos I knew that I wouldn't be able to live at university ... I'm a Muslim my parents weren't too happy with me living by myself and I think it's easier for me as a Muslim to stay at home.

However, it would be wrong to generalise and suggest that this is the only reason why young Muslim women lived with their parents whilst they studied at university. There are other reasons, other values associated with families that were of great importance to some of those we interviewed. For some of these women, remaining at home was a choice, as they valued the day-to-day support that their families could offer. According to Sobia Ali, a Bangladeshi graduate: 'It was okay because it was near home, so I had time to come home as well and had family support there which was really good.'

Whilst the women generally responded positively and agreed with their parents' preferences, some women applied to universities outside their locality against their parents' wishes but were refused permission to leave home. This left some of them frustrated when they were forced to go to universities that they would not otherwise have chosen. In these exceptional cases, we found that these young women were compromising the quality of their education in order to fit in with the preferences of their parents. Saima Mamood, a Pakistani graduate, had a place to study legal executive management at Aston University and was not allowed to go, so she enrolled at Bradford University, studying business management instead. She told us that she regrets not having been allowed to go to Aston as she believes her life would have changed if she had gone there. She is now working in a women's community centre and went on to say that she regrets doing the course she did:

> I was pressurised into either stay local or not go at all so I went to Bradford. I believe I would have been more independent ... I would have been more happier and more proud that I've achieved something I wanted to do ... I regret my career choice. I regret the degree I did to a large extent and now if I can go back in time I would have been more adamant and done law ... my degree didn't really help me.

It was rare that these graduate women had made decisions about attending universities based simply on the university itself or the nature of the course. The location was of major importance. Consequently, the Pakistani and Bangladeshi graduates interviewed in Leeds had applied to local universities such as Huddersfield, Leeds Met, Leeds University, and Bradford University, and those in Birmingham applied to the University of Birmingham, Aston, the University of Central England and Wolverhampton. For these young women, there are local higher education markets, and this makes them a very distinctive as a group of full-time undergraduate students compared to the white middle-class norm. There was no alternative to this; either the women had to choose local universities or risk not having a higher education. Whilst the women did this they were not always happy in retrospect. Humaira Patel, a Pakistani graduate, who had applied only to local universities:

> I would have liked to have gone, but my parents would never agree because they are further away and would not be able to commute ... I would have liked to have attended university further away from home, to experience a more independent living with a more mix of Asian and white people.

In this discussion we have so far focused on the constraints on the choice of undergraduate degrees that emanated from the preferences of some students' parents. However, we did encounter some graduates who faced rather different familial constraints on postgraduate degrees. For example, Jeevan Mudan, an Indian graduate living in Leeds, was single when she left home to go to Brunel University to study for her first degree, as she had a choice: 'I thought I'd go out for a bit, I didn't want to stay at home.' However, by the time of her postgraduate degree she was married and it was difficult for her to leave home, 'I don't think my husband would be too keen on the fact that I'm not home.'

Marriage added another dimension for these women in terms of constraints; it became more difficult for the women to move away when they were married. They talked about their parents' leniency and flexibility, but not all had the same space for negotiation with their husbands. Marriage has often featured as a factor identified in other studies limiting the labour market prospects of South Asian women graduates (Ahmad *et al*, 2003; Dale, *et al* 2002), and we have found that it operates as an important constraint over university choice at undergraduate and postgraduate levels.

Finally, a further unintended negative aspect of the geographical limiting of some of the young women's choices of university is that their preferred degree subject may not be available at all the locally accessible institutions. In a few extreme cases, this would leave the young woman with the choice of one institution that offered a suitable course:

> This was my first choice and my parents would have preferred me to stay at home as opposed to going to like travel away or commute to university or live away from home. They preferred I went to university in my home town which was either Birmingham or Aston and the course that I wanted to do was in Aston so I went there. It was convenient it was local ... you see the degree that I did which was optometry there were about six or seven universities doing it. Aston was the only one that was in Birmingham. And you know I wanted to stay at home my parents preferred me to stay at home. So there wasn't any other university in Birmingham that was doing it. (Khaleda Akmed, Birmingham)

For many of the Bangladeshi and Pakistani young women, there were also constraints associated with working-class origins. These are constraints arising from financial limitations and worries about living independently for the first time and the additional costs that this would bring. These reservations added to the preferences of parents and the expectations of their local communities for choosing local universities:

> My parents didn't feel that I could, well, I don't think they wanted me to go anywhere else, away from home so they said that if I really want to go to university there are two universities in Leeds so they wanted me to apply here. They didn't want me to live away from home because my other brother like I said went to Salford University and was away from home for three years. Well, he would come and visit and everything but they didn't want me to do the same thing because the grant scheme was abolished then and you had to get loans out and my parents didn't want me to be living on loans. They said it would be better for me to stay at home and my brother said the same thing to me as well. That's why I decided to stay at home and go to a local university because I wouldn't need to get loans and things and also from a safety point of view, not having to stay in halls of residents or live in shared student accommodation. (Sobia Ali, Bangladeshi graduate, Leeds)

> I didn't want to actually go away from my mum to be honest, plus I thought if I went away the fact that I wanted to relax because I think when you are living at home (and this has actually proven to be true) because I've been studying with people who are from London and I could see that they have got bills to pay and all these stresses, I had none of that I went home and I slept most of the time or I ate my mum's food and it was really easy that's just how I expected to it to be and I think I made the perfect choice because I wanted to have a relaxing type of thing so. (Fareena Anjum, Pakistani graduate, Leeds)

This theme of not leaving their mothers featured in a number of the young women's accounts of why they actively chose local universities. This often appears to be not only for reasons of emotional attachment to parents, but also out of a sense of duty; as they are becoming adults they feel increasingly obliged to help their parents. For young women, this usually meant housework. In some instances, the young women actively decided to stay at home even if one of their parents were happy for them to move away to study:

> I think it was because of the course that I wanted to do plus I didn't want to go away from home. I always wanted to stay at home because of my mum as she needed me around really. My dad wanted me to go Liverpool but I thought that Bradford was more convenient – I didn't really want to go out and live away from home. (Nargies Khan, Pakistani graduate, Leeds)

> I listed down Birmingham as my second option, Wolverhampton as my first and then it was Westminster and London. But to be honest I got into all of them Westminster was good but then at the end of the day you have to weight up all the options you want to study you don't want to think about your studying you don't want to be paying rent paying bills cause I totally wanted to focus on what I was doing you know in terms of my education cause assignments they come up every so often.

> Interviewer: Would your parents have allowed to you live away from home?

> Yeh they would have, my sister she's in London at the moment and she has been there for about a year now and she is younger than I am and not married so. (Farrah Mughal, Pakistani graduate, Birmingham)

Nevertheless some Pakistani students provided explanations of their localised choices purely in terms of the financial constraints and, perhaps more telling for Muslim students, the fear of debt. This was seen not just in terms of the financial strain on them personally but upon the whole family:

> Well I applied to all the local universities and Aston, UCE and Birmingham are about a twenty minute bus ride. Wolverhampton was the furthest that I was willing to go. If I'd have applied to any of the other universities it would have meant me having to stay there as a resident and that's not something that I wanted to do. I suppose for financial reasons mainly – it would have meant financial restraints; the whole family support system wouldn't be there either and I wasn't comfortable with leaving that. (Iman Karim, Pakistani, Birmingham)

> ... due to financial problems I mean I didn't want to be in loads of debt at the end of my degree. So I did but it was like from where I could commute where I could go on a daily basis. I didn't think about going far. (Shazia Begum, Pakistani, Birmingham)

Sixth formers' plans

So far we have discussed the experiences of those who were currently at university and those who had recently graduated. Broadly speaking, most of the non-Muslim Indian women had some degree of choice about where to study, often basing their decisions, like most middle-class white students (Reay *et al*, 2005), on the best course and institution that they could get into. In contrast, most of the Muslim women experienced some degree of parental or community restriction on where they studied, or just assumed that they would attend a local university as other people like them had done. The question that we address now is whether there are signs that this is changing for younger women, those who are currently in the sixth form.

Among some of the women still studying for their A levels, the question of leaving home also proved to be beyond their control. As for the older Muslim students, it was often thought to be inappropriate for the women to move out of the parental home. For example, Farhana Sheikh, a Pakistani sixth-former, wanted to go to Sheffield to do midwifery. She will have to travel back and forth between Sheffield and Leeds as 'to go and live at Sheffield wouldn't be appropriate, it just wouldn't be an option for my parents to let me'. She explains why: 'they worry cos I'm young and I'm Asian and I'm a girl'. But having said this, she is reluctant to leave home due to the fact that 'I wouldn't feel comfortable'. It is interesting to note in these cases the extent to which some of the women have assimilated their parents' views about these issues. There may indeed be a pattern of expectations becoming established among the younger generation about where it is acceptable to study.

Other young women in the sixth form wanted to stay in their parental home due to the complications of living on their own. In these instances their rationales for staying at home are similar to the White working-class as found in some other studies where monetary constraints are often important. Furthermore, another characteristic that some of these women shared with the white working-class applicants in other studies is the reliance upon the experience of friends (Reay *et al*, 2005). According to Mehwish Begum, a young Pakistani woman:

> finding a home to rent out and staying there will be a hassle. Coming home every weekend will be another hassle, I don't want to go and live somewhere else, I rather stay at home where everything is done for me ... I know when people move out they find it really hard just keeping up with rent and stuff ... it's a personal choice me not wanting to move out ... like it's said nothing's better than home!

Whilst the majority of Pakistani and Bangladeshi women's parents were concerned about their daughters leaving home, it did appear that some of the women did have that choice. Although as we have seen, Mehwish Begum preferred to stay home, she told us that her parents would support her if she decided to move out: 'my parents don't mind where I go, they're like do whatever you want to do'. Khalida Yousaf, a young Bangladeshi also said she had the option of leaving home: 'if I get a place in a good enough university far away and I get into the course I want to do then it is an option they will allow me to go'.

Choosing local universities was where the main difference between the ethnicities emerges amongst the sixth-formers. For the Pakistani sixth-formers in Leeds, for example, there was a strong desire to remain not only within West Yorkshire, but even within Leeds itself. These concerns about morality, parental and community views and the family's *izzat* remain a powerful force among some sections of the Pakistani communities in Leeds and Birmingham. Hajra Khan, a Pakistani sixth-former living in Leeds, who planned to apply to Leeds University had faced difficulties persuading some of her family. She put this down to the values of her Mirpuri community in particular:

> I don't want to go to Bradford; I don't think the family will approve of me going out of the city ... I think it's because with our family there are restrictions ... cos some of the women got spoilt and stuff. They start having relationships with boys and other things. When I came to college, nobody approved of me coming to college, they were like 'we don't want her to ruin the family reputation' and my dad was like 'I have that trust in my daughter and they need to go out cos they are going to step out one day' ... I think it's only in the Mirpuri community because I think with people from the Punjab like Lahore, the parents are educated and then it is passed on, whereas the Mirpuri they don't tend to study.

This underlines the importance of not assuming that all constraints have their source in religion. Different cultures, even from within Pakistan, and different class and educational experiences come into play. It is too simple to assert that Muslim women face constraints. Rather, these constraints are mediated by the need and desire for education, changing values within the communities, and class-related financial limitations as well as cultural diversity amongst Muslims.

It was interesting that most of the women were thinking about applying to local universities, even though in many cases they had not even discussed this with their parents. They knew that it was going to be problematic for them to move out; as Sobia Jabeen, a young Pakistani, simply says, 'I won't be allowed'. Some of the women did not want to push boundaries when it came to their parents; they knew what was acceptable and what was not. It is almost as though the children were protecting their parents from conflict and the possible disapproval of the local community if their daughters moved away.

Conclusions

In this chapter we have looked at the significance of the location of university for South Asian women. Broadly speaking, the parents of most Bangladeshi and Pakistani women prefer their daughters to study at a university near home, preferably within the same city, even when there are several alternatives nearby as is the case in West Yorkshire and the West Midlands. These are partly due to parental perceptions of the risk to the family's *izzat*, but some women felt it was due to religious identification, and there were also financial limitations related to class background.

However, most parents of Indian students do not expect their daughters to remain at home during their undergraduate studies. There is little evidence of this changing, with the pattern apparent among graduates, undergraduates and sixth-formers.

Where to study is very much a family decision for young Bangladeshi and Pakistani women. Some remain with their families for reasons of moral and financial support, whilst others follow their families' preferences. Some of the students and graduates we interviewed experienced some disadvantages such as a limited choice of appropriate courses and missing the experience of personal independence that moving away to university offers.

This is one area where ethnic and religious identity is especially important. The young women clearly appreciated that the cultural constraints on their choice of university were rooted in their ethnic origins and the ways in which these operate for young women. To reject these would have meant rejecting not just their parents, but also their own ethnic and religious identities. Consequently, many of the young women are maintaining their own sense of gendered ethnic or religious self-identity by working within the constraints arising from familial and community preferences. The result is a process of negotiation of what and where to study, and how these plans mesh with expectations about marriage.

It is not possible to predict these outcomes from the young women's ethnicity, religion or class position, or their social or cultural capital. Their interactions with parents and the wider family and community or, as we prefer to refer to it, negotiations in recognition of the relations of power involved, mediate and modify in important ways the preferences of all sides in these decisions.

6

Financial Strategies for Funding a Degree:
the moral economies of family support

The issue of fees and the funding of higher education has been a major national political issue for the past fifteen years or more (Archer *et al*, 2003). Between the early 1960s and the late 1980s, the state paid a student's tuition fees, and living costs were covered by means tested grants and social security payments. However the costs of this system rose in line with the increases both in inflation and in the numbers of undergraduates during the 1980s.

Reflecting the individualist thinking of the 1980s Conservative governments, a new system was introduced where students contributed to the costs of their university education. From 1990 onwards the value of the maintenance grant was frozen, and the remaining costs were to be covered by loans offered to all full-time undergraduates. This loan element increased in proportion to the grant element until 1998. The repayment of the loan began after graduation when the former student was earning 85 per cent of average earnings, and this normally had to be completed within five years (Archer *et al*, 2003; Callender, 2001; Payne and Callender, 1997).

This system was reformed again for those commencing their undergraduate degrees in 1998. In the light of the Dearing Report (Dearing, 1997), full-time university undergraduates now had to contribute up to £1,000 per annum in tuition fees. Furthermore, for those commencing their university education in 1999, loans replaced the grant element entirely, and repayments had to begin once graduates began to earn over £10,000 (Archer *et al*, 2003). Many have commented on the continuity between Conservative and Labour policy over this period. This combination of fees and loans was the funding system experienced by most of the women we interviewed, although it has now been replaced by a system of even higher tuition fees.

There is now a considerable body of research evidence on the different levels of debt and young people's responses to this, much of it based on quantitative surveys of students (Archer *et al*, 2003; Callender, 2001; National Audit Office, 2002; Woodrow *et al*, 2002). Using our interview data, we can throw new light on how a group that is rapidly expanding its participation in university education is coping with the expense that this now entails. We are able to examine Muslim women students' attitudes towards debt, which is seen as *haram* or forbidden by Islam, and compare these to young women of other faiths of South Asian origin. Furthermore, we can examine the expectations of sixth-formers planning to go to university with those who are currently undergraduates or recent graduates.

Another dimension that we are able to consider is the role of the family in providing financial support for students, and how this is creating new patterns of expectations, duty and obligation between the generations and between siblings. Our analysis of the practices or strategies of financial support shows how these are embedded in different moral frameworks.

The changes to the funding of students attending university in the past decade or so have reportedly had negative effects on widening participation (Archer *et al*, 2003; Callender, 2001; Callender, 2003; National Audit Office, 2002; Woodrow *et al*, 2002). Some of this research has reported that South Asian Muslim students are the least likely to take out loans, as just over half of them do so. Such students were more likely to be living with their parents, and spent less than others on leisure activities in pubs, clubs etc. Some have also speculated that Muslim students may refuse to take out loans for religious reasons (Callender and Kemp, 2000: 77). The report by Callender and Kemp also noted that working-class students were more likely to take out loans and to have debts of a higher value. The later study by Callender (2003) found that, among those thinking about going to university, Pakistani Muslims are amongst those who were most averse to debt, with religion being an important factor in determining whether or not students planned to take out a loan.

In the most recent survey of student incomes for 2004-05, Finch *et al* (2006) found that South Asian students had the lowest incomes of any ethnic group, £6,104 per annum compared to £8,531 for black British students. More than half of South Asian students were living with parents: 58% compared to 16% of all students. Their study also revealed that South Asian students were the least likely to take out loans, or to be working whilst studying, and had a low contribution to income from parents although not as low as black students received.

Consequently, we have a good overview of the broad patterns of response to these changes in student finances, including some useful details about their impact on different ethnic groups. However, there is rather less detail on how people from specific social groups plan for and manage their finances as undergraduates. Given the scale of investment and debt that this now involves for individual students and their families, this is a remarkable gap. Here we are obviously limited to considering the diverse strategies used by South Asian women who were undergraduates immediately before the most recent reforms, but these are nevertheless important findings in the context of the ever-changing system of finances for British university students.

The moral economy of students' financial strategies

Despite the increasing volume of research on student finances, there is little attempt to conceptualise how students and their families have responded, these challenges. There are two key ideas which we think can be used to address this issue – the idea of a moral economy, and the idea of strategy. When used to examine the differences between the groups of our sixth-formers, students and recent graduates, we can better understand their responses using these two ideas. Furthermore, this enables us critically to challenge the simplistic market assumptions that lie behind the policy on student fees and loans. The women in our study were not isolated consumers of university degrees, but moral agents seeking to respond creatively to the economic pressure placed upon them and their families.

The term moral economy has been used in social science in a variety of ways (Afshar, 1989a; Sayer, 2004), but in this context we are following Sayer in seeing it as the examination of how morals and norms influence economic behaviour. These may entail assessments of well-being, fairness and justice, but they may equally involve the reproduction of unequal social relationships (Sayer, 2004: 14). Consequently it is important to distinguish different kinds of morals and norms and how they interact with economic forces. For our argument, the consideration of the impact of Islam is especially important, given that taking out loans and paying interest are *haram*. In addition, as we have seen, family support is essential for the young women continuing with their education. Consequently, their families' financial support also has a moral and ethical dimension.

Nevertheless, morals and norms are open to contest, interpretation and change, so that one cannot mechanically link economic behaviour to moral commitments. Furthermore, moral objections to loans, for example, might be overwhelmed by economic necessity. As we shall see, there are different moral rationalities in play for different groups of students in how they approach the planning of their educational finances.

The second idea that we wish to draw upon is the concept of strategy, which refers to the way in which people take account of others' expectations of them when making decisions (Elster, 1979: 18-19). This is a quite specific use of the concept of strategy, which has been used in a diverse range of ways by different social scientists (Crow, 1989).

For us, strategy refers to how students develop their financial plans with a consideration of the expectations of and longer term consequences for their families and themselves. One can see at once how moral and ethical concerns enter into these strategies. We are not suggesting that the young South Asian women whom we interviewed were being strategic in a purely economically rational way. Rather, they were being morally and ethically strategic with respect to their culture, religion, families and future economic well-being. Their strategies were thus embedded in moral economies of religion, culture and kin and the expectations and responses that arise from these.

Furthermore, these varied according to different groups of women, thus highlighting the ethnic, religious and class diversity among the broader pan-ethnic category of South Asian. In this way, they were often trying to preserve some established cultural and religious ways of organising economic life, by not taking out loans for example, whilst engaging with a system of student finance that required them to operate in an individualistic and calculating manner. Their response entailed thinking and acting strategically in that they had to take account of their families' expectations of them in making their decisions.

Sixth formers

We begin our discussion with those who were currently in the sixth form when we interviewed them in order to examine their financial plans for university. Most of the 16-18 year old students we interviewed had given little thought to how they would fund their university education. Many assumed that there would be a combination of support from their parents, student loans and their own part-time employment. As Hajra Khan, a Pakistani A level student in Leeds, told us: 'I know I have the support of my parents or probably

112

student loan'. Others were planning to work now and save money to pay for their university education:

> I've been told that if I get a job now, to save a bit for when I get to university. I will also have the loan, so because it is only a three year course it won't be as bad as a five year course. (Saira Begum, Bangladeshi sixth-former)

In a very few instances, Muslim A level students were opposed to taking out a loan on the grounds that they are *haram* in Islam. This was the reason given by Zarqa Aslam, a Bangladeshi A level student in Leeds: 'Cos at the end you'll have to pay it all back with interest added on it and in Islam we're not allowed to pay interest.' However, this was the exception among the Muslim students of all ages.

Many of the 16-18 year olds were currently in receipt of Education Maintenance Allowances (EMAs) designed to help the children of low-income families continue into further education. Many were in receipt of the highest level, £30 per week. For example, Rupreet Kaur, a Sikh student studying for GNVQs at an FE college in Birmingham, told us: 'I get EMA, that's thirty pounds a week the money I get for college'. EMAs seemed to be a significant source of financial support easing the strain on family resources as the young women studied for the necessary A levels or GNVQs required for entry to university. Some sixth-formers were unaware of the real costs of a university education until we told them during the interview, and were genuinely shocked, expecting support from the government:

> I'm working now, so I think working will support me. I didn't think it cost that much. Doesn't the government help you out at my age? (Anela Hussain, Pakistani sixth-former)

Overall, the picture amongst the sixth-formers concerning their plans for financing their degrees is one of uncertainty, and they assumed that they would continue to be dependent upon their parents. As found in other studies (Callender, 2003), they often had unduly optimistic expectations about their future finances at university. One consequence of the changes to the student finance system since the early 1990s has thus been to add a new layer of dependence to the relationship between South Asian female students and their parents. The sixth-formers generally assumed that their parents would continue to support them in their university education, and as their parents wanted the best for them this was generally the case. This theme of continued financial dependency upon parents is one that we now consider in our discussion of undergraduates and recent graduates.

Undergraduates and graduates

Among undergraduates and graduates, it is possible to identify a range of financial strategies for funding university education. In individual cases, however, these are not always mutually exclusive. Nevertheless, for the vast majority of the young women who were recent graduates or who were currently at university, their strategies fitted largely into one category or another. Each of these can be thought of analytically as distinct strategies embedded in different moral economies.

Table 6.1: Typology of students' financial strategies

Mixed economy of loans, wages and parental support
Rejection of loans due to religious objections or risk
Using loans as an insurance
Dependence on parents
Independence from parents
Support from siblings and the extended family
State benefits
Reliance on part-time work

Those currently at university typically had a strategy of drawing upon a wide range of sources for their income, typically a mix of loans, part-time employment and support from parents. In this respect they are very like other undergraduates, as reported in more general studies of student finance (Finch *et al*, 2006). However, many were relying on more parental support by living at home as well as receiving money directly from parents. Davinder Kaur, a Sikh student in Leeds, described a typical set of arrangements:

> I've got a loan and my parents help me out a lot. My parents pay my course fees and then I use my loan to live off and my wages. Usually every term they'll give me a lump sum to help me out.

Only a minority of the current undergraduates expressed an aversion to taking out loans. As noted earlier, only a few Muslim students did not take out loans because they are *haram*. In these cases they received additional support from their parents, or they had different financial plans for their university education:

> We didn't take out a loan as it had interest on it and in Islam interest is forbidden so there was no point getting something and you have to pay back with interest at the

end so whatever happens my mum and dad said 'we'll help you out.' (Rahila Akhtar, Indian Muslim undergraduate in Leeds)

Well to be honest the whole loan thing ... if I do my midwifery I wouldn't – personally I wouldn't go in to uni again and take a loan out knowing that that's *haram* now. As in at the time I didn't know at the time that taking out a loan on interest is *haram*. So personally even if did, knowing that midwifery I wouldn't have to take a loan out because they would pay you, give you a bursary, what you don't pay back for it. So that would be okay for me. But if I did do another course I wouldn't be taking out the loan anyway and then I wouldn't have any debt. (Farhana Sheikh, Pakistani)

Another strategy for financial management was to obtain a student loan but not to use the money except in times of exceptional need. This was the strategy of using loans as a kind of insurance that was particularly found among Muslim students due to their aversion to getting into debt. They would have preferred not to have to take out loans, but most found they had to draw upon them at some point. Shazia Begum, a Bangladeshi undergraduate in Leeds, explained to us that: 'I have taken out a loan but I haven't used it. It's in case if I might need it or something or need extra money'.

The debts of current students and graduates ranged from zero to £18,000, with many of the young women reporting debts of between £9,000 to £10,000 regardless of religion or whether or not they were living away from home. The highest level of debt of £18,000 was reported by a Pakistani Muslim graduate, who had lived away from her parents' home as both an undergraduate and as a postgraduate student. Other students told us that they avoided debt because of the negative experiences of older siblings. Bushra Kauser from Birmingham also indicated that parents and some siblings often felt obliged to help their daughters to avoid debt.

It does seem, then, that the newer systems of student finance are creating difficulties for whole families as well as new relationships of obligation and dependence between parents and children, as parents help their younger children after seeing their older siblings get into serious debt. As Bushra explained:

My brother took out a loan he's got over £21,000 debt, he's only just got married, Sadia my eldest sister only took out a loan twice for two fees – she was in £7k debt. She's got a job now so she can begin to pay it back. My mum was like 'you are not going through that' and my sister was 'no we are not having you in debt if you need any money I will support you.'

Another important way in which relationships with parents operated with respect to financing a university education was the sense of guilt that some of the women felt at continuing to be dependent upon their parents or other relatives. This is what we mean when we speak of new emergent relationships of obligation and duty being produced between the generations, and these were exemplified in the strategy of dependence upon parents. These do not appear to be without moral or emotional strain for the young women. In this sense, the financial decisions of the young women are rooted in moral frameworks which are cultural rather than religious in their origin. They recognise the other obligations that their relatives have or their sheer inability to help them:

> I have a student loan, my granddad would have paid for it but I didn't want him to be bled dry for my school fees and he has other responsibilities through his children, all their schooling as well as everything else. So I've got a loan, only £3,000 for my rent for the year and then I did work a bit in my first term. And then my granddad helps me too, he puts a bit in my account every week which he has only started doing recently. And my dad sends me money every quarter. (Sadia Hussain)

> My parents have not given me a bulk of so many thousand to help me along, which is because I have not expected it from them, my parents aren't well off. This money that I use from the loan company, I can pay back from my salary that I am going to get in the future. I don't want my family to finance me like that, they're not well off. (Fatima Begum)

For these Muslim students, then, the use of loans arose from their own concerns about the impact of paying for higher education out of their family's finances. There were, however, a range of other financial strategies among the young women that we interviewed that were, perhaps in part, grounded in this moral fear of dependence on parents, or the guilt associated with being financially dependent on parents. One of these was to seek total financial independence from parents. Samreen, a Pakistani graduate and Mandeep, an Indian undergraduate, are extreme examples of this type of strategy. However, this autonomy carries with it the price of increased levels of debt:

> Financially I didn't accept a penny off my parents. I refused. I wouldn't take any money off my brothers or off my parents. I fought them every step of the way. And I think that for me was really important because I needed to get and I needed to know that I was independent and that I was doing it on my own. Not cos I want to be able to say I've done it on my own but just to be able to know that I can. (Samreen Patel)

> My parents have always ... offered you know to help me but I never took a penny off them. Because I'd rather stand on my own two feet and see what life's like. I'd rather not, if I do get stuck then fair enough I would go to them but then I would rather stand on my own two feet and fall back down and learn from my mistakes. (Mandeep Kaur)

At the other extreme were a few instances where parents maintained control over their daughters' finances. Beenish, a Sikh student in Birmingham, was one of the clearest examples of this type of strategy. Her father had strongly advised her not to take out a loan, and, as she went on to tell us:

> I'm not good with handling money you know. I've had all my credit cards taken off me so I only get cash now. So until I can prove to my dad that I can spend wisely am not allowed to have one.

> Interviewer: Who gives you spending money?

> It's so embarrassing I'm 20 but I still get spending money off my dad. I work weekends and I only get £80 £90 a week so I don't spend that it goes in an account for the future.

Although almost all of the young women whom we interviewed reported on some kind of parental support, some told us that their husbands, brothers and sisters were also providing support. In some cases, the support from siblings seemed to be especially important, and this is why it merits treatment as a separate strategy of support from the wider family grounded in a moral economy of kinship. In these cases, the whole financial resources of the wider family are mobilised to support the education of the young woman, which demonstrates that the families' and the wider community's commitment to the university education of the daughters is very substantial indeed. Jameela Yaqoob, a Bangladeshi student in Leeds, told us:

> Whenever I am going home my brother is always giving me money and recently I've been short of money so he gives me an allowance of about £50 per week which is fine by me. He has supported me a lot, when I'm short of paying my rent and stuff he pays.

Most of the women who were currently at university were working part-time in some way, and most of the recent graduates had also worked during their studies. One particular strategy was to work in several jobs, or to work long hours during the summer holiday. As Bushra Kauser, a Sikh undergraduate in Birmingham, explained:

> When I was working over summer I was working full-time in the holidays so I was working for a few weeks because of my brother's wedding they wouldn't give me time off but I made about £800 in that three weeks it was completely full-time so I was working my arse off.

Finally, there is the strategy of using state benefits to fund a university education. This obviously means that any young woman using this strategy has to meet the criteria of eligibility for those benefits. For example, Zoreena Bibi, a

Bangladeshi graduate in Leeds who started her degree when she was 24, explained how she had relied on state benefits during her time at university as a mother:

> I financed my degree because I was on income support 80 per cent of the fees were paid and 20 per cent I paid which wasn't much and the second degree the post-graduate I had to finance it fully. It was a struggle but I looked for funding but they said studying for a higher education like masters is a privilege you should be able to finance it yourself.

This last case raises the issue of financing postgraduate qualifications. We interviewed several women who were either contemplating or actually studying for postgraduate qualifications, and in some instances this would lead to additional financial strains. As Fatima Begum, a Bangladeshi student in Leeds, who was considering training in Birmingham to become a solicitor and already had debts of £12,000 told us:

> That is going get higher though with my LPC, because I would have to invest £12,000 on my own. £8,000 for the course and then £4,000 for living in Birmingham – £2,000 for rent and £2,000 living.

Most current undergraduates and recent graduates drew upon a mixed economy of financial support for their higher education from loans, parents and siblings and their own employment. Direct financial support from parents and even the wider family was especially important for almost all of the current undergraduates whom we interviewed, and this seems to be creating new layers of obligation and dependence between parents and their offspring. There was little aversion to the necessity of using student loans. Refusal to take out loans was found to a limited extent among a few Muslim students, but among Sikh and Hindu students this was also based upon the negative experiences of older siblings and the advice of parents. Debts ranged from zero to £18,000 and they were owed not only to the Student Loans Company, but also credit cards, bank overdrafts and loans and friends.

Finally despite the strong desire to pursue further qualifications, the self-financing of postgraduate qualifications was especially difficult. This last feature is likely to be a significant source of further educational inequality in the future as many more people graduate with first degrees.

Conclusion

In this chapter we have examined the diverse financial strategies of South Asian women in the sixth form, as well as those currently at university or who have recently graduated. We have used the idea of a moral economy and strategy to analyse how the young women were taking account of the family members' expectations of them as rooted in their cultural assumptions and religious beliefs. However, many of those in the sixth form contemplating university seemed to be poorly informed about the financial demands of going to university and they were vague about their own financial planning. Furthermore, a significant number of them were reliant upon Education Maintenance Allowances at the full value of £30 per week.

At the time of writing, another new system of student finance is in the process of being introduced for those commencing their undergraduate education in 2006. This combines a new, much higher fee of £3,000 per year with a system of bursaries and other forms of support. Whilst one of the major criticism of the old system was that it was excessively complex (Archer *et al*, 2003), the fact that universities may vary their fees and each institution has its own system of bursaries in addition to other forms of support merely makes the system even more complex and confusing for all.

It remains to be seen what effects the most recent changes to student finance will have on this picture. Obvious issues for future research include the impact of the move to £3,000 per annum fees and the market of discounts and bursaries on student and parental choices among South Asian communities. The take-up of bursaries should be carefully monitored to see if there are any emergent patterns of inequality related to ethnic origin, sex and social class background. What can be certain is that young South Asian women at university will be responding strategically in the light of their families' financial limitations, moral commitments and religious beliefs.

7

Racism, Islamophobia and Experiences of University

One of the main purposes of this chapter is to challenge the enduring liberal myth that universities as seats of academic learning are somehow insulated from racist practices and behaviour (Bird, 1996). Although this has been systematically challenged in a number of ways, through the demonstration of institutional racism and the cultural bias of academic life (Carter *et al*, 1999; Law *et al*, 2004; Read *et al*, 2003), the day-to-day experiences of ethnic minority students are poorly understood.

Whilst there is a considerable literature analysing ethnic minority patterns of application to universities, including South Asian women, the literature on their experiences as students is much more limited (Bird, 1996; Clarke, 2000; Housee, 2004). Other studies of students' sense of belonging or isolation at university have been more general, encompassing class differences as well as a broad range of ethnic minority groups, and have focused upon relationships with the broader academic culture rather than experiences of racism (Bird, 1996; Read *et al*, 2003).

Research carried out in the early 1990s into black students' experiences of higher education found that ethnic minority students were often isolated both as individuals amongst predominately white students, and as students being taught by predominantly white staff. In such circumstances, students often reported experiences of discriminatory attitudes and behaviour from both university staff and students (Bird, 1996: 22-5).

Although Carter *et al* (1999) focused on the employment of ethnic minorities in universities, they also completed some limited qualitative research with a small number of ethnic minority graduate students. This found that ethnic minority graduate students felt themselves to be stereotyped by white academics, and that they did not fit into the dominant academic culture. In the USA research has also produced evidence of parallel experiences amongst African-American students at predominantly white universities (Feagin *et al*, 1996).

Clarke (2000), in his study of ethnic minority undergraduates, found that there was a continuity of experiences of racism from school through to higher education. However, once at university, ethnic minority students also had a powerful sense of not belonging, of hidden discrimination and of being made to feel unwelcome by other students and staff. Racism is both institutional and personal and has a powerful emotional dimension in both how it is expressed and people's experiences of it (Clarke, 2000).

In comparison to this lack of research into the experiences of racism in British higher education, there is now a considerable literature on the experiences, views and identities of South Asian girls at school (Abbas, 2004; Bhatti, 1999; Shain, 2003), as well as the everyday racism, such as name-calling experienced by ethnic minority children more generally in schools (Connolly, 1998; Troyna, 1987; Troyna and Hatcher, 1992; Wright, 1992), other spaces such as youth clubs (Back, 1996), and the general experiences of ethnic minority people of racial harassment (Modood *et al*, 1997).

Racist name-calling can be a key event in peoples' lives, when they first become aware of racism and the assumptions of some white people about them (Bird, 1996; Phoenix, 2005). In a recent study of Bradford schools, for example, Din (2006) found that up to 50 per cent of his sample of Pakistani pupils reported being bullied, often with a racist element. The majority of the girls in Shain's (2003) study also reported racist name-calling. In relation to South Asian girls, this has been conceptualised as sexual othering (Brah and Minhas, 1985; Connolly, 1998; Shain, 2003), where they are seen as either passive or exotic, unknowable and unpredictable by dominant white society.

Since the riots in northern towns in 2001 (Bagguley and Hussain, 2005; Hussain and Bagguley, 2005), the September 11 attacks on New York and other global political events, Muslim women in particular have become increasingly visible as members of a feared and vilified minority (Abbas, 2005; Shain, 2003). Official reports of racist incidents have increased significantly since 1999/2000, when 2,417 individuals were reported to police for racist incidents, and by 2004/2005 this had grown to 5,788, an increase of over 100 per cent. The year 2004/2005 was the first year that national level data on religiously aggravated crime was recorded, and 67 per cent of this was directed at Muslims (Crown Prosecution Service, 2005).

These figures are mirrored in the data on people's perceptions of racism and religious prejudice in Britain. This shows that, since 2000, most people think that there is now more racial prejudice than in the past, and that South Asian people and Muslims are the main targets. Muslim women reported the highest levels of perception of religious prejudice, and people of Bangladeshi and Pakistani origin felt that it had increased the most. In the same survey in 2005, over 90 per cent of all respondents felt that religious prejudice against Muslims had increased.

Muslims and Sikhs were twice as likely as other religious groups to have reported discrimination on the basis of religion by government organisations, and Muslims were five times more likely to have reported discrimination in employment on the basis of religion (Department for Communities and Local Government, 2006). Although such figures should not be treated as definitive due to problems in recording these types of incident (Modood *et al*, 1997: 262-4), the trend they depict is unequivocal.

These events and the wider political responses to them form an essential backdrop to our discussions of the young women's experiences of racism. Our research design has enabled us to examine experiences of racism and xeno-phobia for different ethnic and religious groups and in different locations inside and outside the university. Rather than there being a generic ethnic minority or black experience of higher education as suggested in some litera-ture (Ball *et al*, 2002; Bird, 1996; Read *et al*, 2003), the positioning of South Asian Muslims in particular by recent global and local political events re-quires a significant re-thinking of this approach.

This chapter considers the experiences of the women at university where they are often a visible ethnic minority. For some they will be the only South Asian women on their course. Here we find that some young women found the transition to university quite stressful as they were often moving from a situa-tion at school or sixth form where South Asian women were part of either a majority or a substantial minority, to a situation at university where they may be part of a small minority or even isolated and alone. Whilst the emergence of certain universities and types of course having disproportionate numbers of ethnic minority students has often been commented upon (Connor *et al*, 2004; Modood, 1993; Reay *et al*, 2005; Taylor, 1993a; 1993b) there is a com-parative lack of discussion of the students' experiences of this.

We then go on to look at their experiences of what they defined as racism. This discussion is divided into several parts. Firstly, we look at how far they felt that they fitted in at university. How far did they feel that university was a place for people like themselves? How did they cope with being in a largely white environment? Secondly, we examine their experiences of racism outside of education, the specific impact of 9/11 and Islamophobia, their memories of racism at school or in the sixth form, and finally their experiences of racism at university.

Explaining racism in universities

Previous studies of ethnic minority students' experiences of racism at university have highlighted issues of social isolation and the whiteness of the institutions in terms of their culture, staffing and student body (Bird, 1996; Clarke, 2000; Feagin *et al*, 1996; Puwar, 2004). From these studies, two accounts of racism in universities have emerged. Puwar (2004) draws upon Bourdieu's analogy of the 'fish out of water', suggesting that those with ethnic minority identities do not fit in with the white cultural norms of the university. Thus, ethnic minority staff are subject to extra surveillance by management in universities. Although Puwar is concerned with university academic staff, her argument could equally apply to students.

Clarke's approach is grounded in psychoanalysis. He explains racism partly in terms of universities reflecting the racism of wider society, and also at the interpersonal level, as white students and staff project their own stereotypes and anxieties onto ethnic minority students. The students concerned often find it difficult to explain their feelings of not belonging at university, of being outsiders and being made to feel uncomfortable (Clarke, 2000).

Some of these studies have overlooked the gendered dynamics of racism, especially as they apply to South Asian women as suggested by other authors (Brah and Minhas, 1985; Connolly, 1998; Shain, 2003). Furthermore, they have often failed to make sufficient distinction between the racisms directed at different ethnic groups, and of particular importance here is the rise of Islamophobia in universities (Tyrer, 2004). It is also important to examine how far different social contexts might be felt to be more or less racist by ethnic minority students, or where there are sufficient numbers of ethnic minority students to develop a viable collective resistance to racism in the university. Survey evidence has shown how the level of harassment is lower in the geographical areas which have a higher percentage of ethnic minority residents (Modood *et al*, 1997: 271).

Finally, these studies of racism within higher education have often been inadequately contextualised in relation to wider political events. For our study, the young women's experiences of racism and Islamophobia were profoundly affected by responses to the 2001 riots in the North of England and the 9/11 attacks in New York.

In our analysis, we have adapted the concept of 'critical mass' from feminist studies of the effect of women's increasing participation in politics (Dahlerup, 1988; Lovenduski, 2001) and in the workplace (Kanter, 1977), in order to think about how far experiences of racism may vary across different contexts and to explore the possibilities of collective support and resistance against racism. The idea of critical mass refers to the situation when the size of a minority social group in an institution reaches a certain level – a critical mass. The social character of that institution then changes markedly as the minority group can begin to have a noticeable effect on how the institution is run. Generally it is assumed that around 30 per cent is the threshold of a critical mass (Lovenduski, 2001: 744).

However, our point is rather different. We suggest that, when a critical mass of ethnic minority students is reached in a university or degree course, the experience of ethnic minority students is likely to change markedly. They are less likely to feel like a 'fish out of water' (Puwar, 2004), and the university is likely to seem to be more welcoming to them. This draws upon Kanter's (1977) analysis of the experiences of women in American corporations where she found that when women were a token minority, generally less than 15 per cent, the men were more likely to exaggerate the differences between men and women. This entailed the use of sexist jokes, constant reminders of women being different and out of place, and the isolation of women in work groups, etc.

This has parallels with Clarke's (2000) psychoanalytic analysis of racism in universities and its emotional impact. This approach is also congruent with empirical findings on the lower levels of racial harassment reported from those places with higher densities of ethnic minority residents (Modood *et al*, 1997: 271). As we shall see, something like this happened to those young South Asian women who were in a minority in their course or university.

On being in a mixed environment

At the national level several authors have noted the strong tendency for new universities in particular to have a higher than expected percentage of ethnic minority students (Connor *et al*, 2004; Modood, 1993; Reay *et al*, 2005; Shiner and Modood, 2002; Taylor, 1993a; 1993b). However, they note that not all new universities or former polytechnics fall into this category. Indeed, more recent evidence shows that some old universities have a higher percentage of ethnic minority students (see table 7.1 below).

The interviews in Leeds were carried out with women who were attending both Leeds University and Leeds Metropolitan University; there was a vast difference in their experience of the institutions in terms of race and ethnicity. Those studying at Leeds University found themselves in a predominantly white environment whereas those at Leeds Metropolitan University experienced a more ethnically mixed institution.

The table opposite provides details of the ethnic composition of the student bodies in those institutions that most of our interviewees attended. Whilst these show little difference between the two main universities in Leeds, the concentration of South Asian students in particular courses at Leeds Metropolitan University, as well as that university's positive image among ethnic minorities, affected those students' experiences in a positive way. Within the West Midlands institutions there tended to be higher proportions of South Asian students. Particularly noticeable in this respect is the University of Aston. This reflects the higher proportion of South Asian people living in the region as well as the types of courses offered at different institutions and the tendency, especially of South Asian women, to study at a local university.

For those at Leeds University, the shift to a white environment did have an impact on some of the students. They described the emotional effects of being a fish out of water. For instance, according to Isha Sharma, an Indian undergraduate: 'I wasn't used to seeing so many white people in one area!' Jameela Yaqoob, a Bangladeshi Muslim, reiterated such sentiments: 'when I first came to uni I thought oh my god where are all the Asians? I couldn't see any Asians, and my courses especially and I was thinking where the hell are they?' The importance of having other Muslim Asians around her was highlighted by Jameela Yaqoob further on in the conversation when she told us that: 'you can be more open and you just feel more confident because you know you speak the same things and you're in a similar situation'. This highlights the point about critical mass, of being able to share experiences with others who have similar identities and culture. When there is such a critical mass, this turns the whole experience of being at university from being a negative, stressful one to one that is much more positive.

However, for some of the women, the issue of ethnic difference was raised for them by the reactions of the white people that they encountered at university.

Table 7.1: UK domiciled students by gender and ethnic group for universities in or near the study areas 2003-04

Ethnicity	Gender	Leeds	LMU	Birmingham	Aston	UCE	Wolverhampton
White	Female	50.6%	44.3%	36.8%	26.3%	41.8%	43.5%
	Male	36.3%	34.5%	25.6%	27.2%	23.5%	24.9%
Black	Female	0.9%	1.3%	1.6%	1.8%	7.1%	4.2%
	Male	0.6%	1.2%	0.9%	1.5%	3.4%	2.2%
Asian	Female	3.1%	3.6%	5.9%	19.3%	9.5%	8.9%
	Male	2.6%	4.7%	5.0%	19.8%	9.9%	8.3%
Other	Female	1.5%	0.8%	1.2%	1.3%	1.9%	1.2%
	Male	0.9%	0.7%	0.8%	1.3%	0.9%	0.7%
Unknown	Female	1.9%	5.0%	12.9%	0.5%	1.1%	3.1%
	Male	1.6%	3.8%	9.2%	1.0%	1.0%	3.0%
TOTAL		100.0%	100.0%	100.0%	100.0%	100.0%	100.0%

Source: Higher Education Statistics Agency

Some white students had never personally known South Asian people before, and brought certain stereotypes with them to these first encounters. These stereotypes typically involved the sexual othering of South Asian women as passive and docile, domesticated and subjugated, as noted by previous researchers (Brah and Minhas, 1985; Connolly, 1998; Shain, 2003). Within education this is also sometimes presented in terms of their being expected by staff to be destined for marriage (Bhatti, 1999; Bird, 1996: 21).

According to Davinder Kaur, an Indian undergraduate at Leeds University, some white people were surprised to see her at university. Davinder went on to talk about the problems associated with this, where some of her fellow white students assumed that all South Asian women do not drink and socialise in the same way as young white people. They had a stereotype of a typical Indian girl as domesticated and compliant. Davinder described one of these encounters in the following way:

> When I interact with people I don't think I'm a brown girl and you're a white man, but it was other people that made me aware. It was like 'wow, look at you, I've never met an Indian person before'. I said 'I can't be a representative for all Indian people. I'm one experience of it.' They said 'wow but you go out drinking, you're not typical'. I said 'how can you say that what is a typical Indian girl?' They had this image of a girl that stands in the kitchen.

This kind of experience is typical of situations where the women constituted a tokenistic minority on their course or at their university. As Kanter (1977: 208) puts it when writing about women in overwhelmingly male organisations, they are not treated as individuals but as symbols of the minority that they come from. One response to this situation where you are one of a tokenistic minority is to seek out contact with others similar to yourself in order to overcome the sense of social isolation. Some of the South Asian women had more contact with other South Asians as a result of going to a university or studying on a course with a critical mass of ethnic minority students from a similar background.

Simi Banu, an Indian undergraduate currently studying English at university, who comes from a predominantly Sikh neighbourhood in the West Midlands, only had a few Sikh friends prior to coming to university. On her course she was one of very few South Asian women. Although now she finds herself in an environment which is predominately white, she has found that she has far more contact with other South Asian students. Simi feels she has learnt more about her Indian roots and the diversity among South Asians as a result of being at university, as she explained to us:

> At home I have two Indian friends the rest are all white. In contrast to here no one can believe I live with four Indian women here! We are so different ... we have been to each other's family homes for 21st birthdays ... you think 'wow' we are all Indian, but we are all so different!

In these cases, a common ethnic and religious identity, shared experiences and understandings seemed to provide these students with important sources of support in the white social space of the university. This highlights the importance of there being a sufficient number in a minority for them to form meaningful networks of mutual support, hence the importance of critical mass. These circumstances turn the experience of university into a positive one. For instance, Fatima Begum, a Bangladeshi Muslim, deliberately chose South Asian friends at university:

> Most of my social circle is in the Asian community, I mean I can speak to my white friends up until certain point ... but there is more of common understanding between you and your Asian friend. You talk about things that are a bit more deeper and your friendship is more deeper because you feel as though they understand you ... I don't want to make more white friends but I do have white friends.

Among those who had graduated, there had been similar issues for these women who had experienced an environment where there were many people from their own ethnicity, but had now moved into an educational environment that was predominantly, even overwhelmingly white. This is something they clearly remember about going to university and the shock stays with them after graduation. For instance, Rahila Akhtar a Pakistani graduate, initially had problems coming to Leeds: 'I went to a school where there was a lot more Asians about 60/40 so going to Leeds was a bit of a shock.'

In a similar way, the ethnic composition of particular degree courses may be more important than the ethnic composition of the whole university's student body. Whilst there may be a critical mass of South Asian students at the level of the whole institution, on a day-to-day basis students experience life in the lectures and seminars of their own degree course. For example, Saima Mamood, a Pakistani graduate in Birmingham, found it hard being the only Asian girl on her course, although there were a lot of South Asian students at her university as a whole:

> The school I went to was predominately Asian and I mean you go from one extreme to another. At the beginning it was an issue but towards the end it wasn't an issue because we all just got on with our degree.

However, there were others who refused to look at this kind of experience in a negative way. For instance, Fareena, a Pakistani graduate, came from an area of predominately South Asian people and then went into university where she was the one of two Asian women on the course, but she told us that she relied on the fact that she could seek support at home:

> I found this ok, if I wanted my own cultural people or whatever I'd go home, you get enough of that so I don't really mind it just makes life more interesting, so I don't really think too much of it ... people will find it a bit difficult to say my name but that's about it

In this section we have outlined the women's responses to moving to different kinds of ethnic environments. In many cases, students experienced a sense of surprise or shock in the first instance as they noted that there were so few South Asian people at their university or on their course compared to the schools and sixth forms that they had attended previously. Many were the only student from their background on their course, and some of these women found this to be a particularly isolating experience. Many maintained strong friendships with other South Asian women and for some these were an especially strong source of support in overwhelmingly white environments. Some experienced quite explicit racist and sexist stereotypes about South Asian women from their fellow white students, and we explore the young women's experiences of racism in more detail in the following sections.

Experiences of racism and Islamophobia in public places

Experiences of racism directed towards them in public places were described to us by a number of the young women. The forms of racist behaviours varied from physical attacks to verbal abuse based upon negative cultural assumptions, especially about the gendered character of South Asian culture. Much of the racism was in the form of Islamophobia, and many non-Muslim students experienced this, as many white non-Muslims apparently assume that all South Asians are Muslims. Whilst none of the women said that they had complained formally to their universities, those who had complained at school or college had been ignored. The racism in universities seemed to be most frequently encountered in those institutions and courses with very small numbers of ethnic minority students.

Many of the women we interviewed talked about experiencing verbal comments from white men in particular, and much of this explicit verbal racism was in public places, workplaces and the areas where the young women lived. As clothing is often seen as an ethnic marker for many South Asian women, those who wore headscarves (*hijab*), with its connotations for some white people of what they believe is the traditionalism and backwardness of South Asian Muslims, tended to experience the most explicit and extreme forms of racism and Islamophobia. Zoreena Bibi, a Bangladeshi graduate, experienced this kind of racism in one of her jobs as a receptionist:

> Once where I worked as a receptionist I was wearing *hijab*. They just assumed I couldn't read. It was sort of like reading a notice in front of me and they were just slowly reading it and I put it there so that didn't make no sense so they think you're backward if you wear a *hijab*.

However racism did not just take the form of verbal comments or behaving in ways that assumed the young women wearing the *hijab* did not understand English. Saydhah Shah, an Indian Muslim graduate, told us how she was subjected to both verbal and physical abuse by white men at a bus stop when she was younger:

> It was at high school, I stayed over after class when everyone else had left so when I went to the bus stop, it was in quite a white area with a big council estate heavily populated by white people, and I was just standing alone at the bus stop and there were a few white guys who started giving me verbal abuse they then started throwing bottles at me. I was quite scared ... I basically I just stood at the bus stop till my bus came.

Racism experienced in public areas outside of universities is still important as it affects the lives of these students. Saydhah Shah told us how she had also experienced comments on the way to university when she was a student in Leeds. The way in which she dismissively talks about these events reveals how they are an almost taken-for-granted aspect of everyday experience in British society:

> When I first started, it was my first day and someone went past and said 'ooh, you wear a scarf because you've got nits in your hair?' ... I don't really think they were university students, I just think they were passing through, a few lads.

Fareena Anjum, a Pakistani student in Leeds, used to live in a predominately white area where her family was subjected to racist attacks by their neighbours for several years. These experiences of racist harassment in residential areas reflect those widely reported in other research (Modood *et al*, 1997). In Fareena's case these only came to an end when more South Asian families moved into the street and there were complaints about the neighbours:

> We moved into our house it was an all white area and you know we used to have our house trashed and phone wires cut and cars smashed up and fences down and garage beaten down and all sorts of stuff yeah for about two years egg on the house and everything ...

The Bangladeshi and the Indian women talked about being called 'Pakis', especially when they had been at school or in public spaces. The word has become a generic term of racist abuse directed at all South Asians. Ironically the label 'Paki' to the women would mean Pakistani, according to Jameela Yaqoob, a Bangladeshi student: 'I've been called Paki, but you think 'well, I'm not a Paki so why are you calling me a Paki? They seem to call everyone a Paki.' The Bangladeshi and Indian women would take most offence to this particular type of racist name-calling. According to several Bangladeshi and Indian students, this used to be common in the schools that they had attended:

> Even though we're not Pakis we get called Pakis. We used to get called that a lot in school but it has calmed down a lot now and they have kind of like realised that we're not all the same. (Nalufa Begum, Bangladeshi sixth-former, Leeds)

> When you're called something you're not like Paki, it's quite offensive and when people ask you what you are, I say am an Indian then they come out and say are you Muslim? I'll be like no I'm not! (Bina Muckerjee, Indian undergraduate, Leeds)

> People called us Pakis even though were not Pakistani. I'm not a Pakistani I'm Bangladeshi but they would always label us as Pakistani and used certain words to describe us. (Sobia Ali, Bangaldeshi graduate, Leeds)

For the most part, these incidents in public places took place before attendance at university and were unconnected with it. They are nevertheless important as defining experiences for the women concerned. For the first time, they experience directly how some white people see them (Bird, 1996; Phoenix, 2005). However, in other cases they experienced racism travelling to and from university or whilst out socialising with friends from university. In one case, this had contributed to one student changing her university from Durham to Leeds after she had started her degree:

> There was an incident in Durham where someone spat at me in the street and I was so mad, I wanted to go after him and thump him and my friends had to stop me. I was so angry and I was screaming and swearing and my friends said, look you've got to calm down, just leave it, it's not worth it ... I was like, you come and do that to my face and see what you get back. I can't believe that people exist in the world that think I'm less than them because I'm not white. (Davinder Kaur, Indian undergraduate, Leeds)

Davinder's experiences highlight the significance of the emotional impact of experiences of explicit racism (Clarke, 2000). It also illustrates the importance of experiences outside the university, and the impact that these can have on students' education. Universities are not insulated from the effects of wider racism in society.

9/11 and Islamophobia

The fieldwork for this research took place after the attacks in the US in September 2001. Some of the women suffered from the backlash of 9/11, especially those who wore the *hijab*. Housee (2004), for instance, has documented the perception amongst Muslim students of the increased Islamophobia and tensions between students since then. Otherwise, much of the debate about the impact of 9/11 on university campuses has been framed in terms of the search for Islamic fundamentalism that targets Muslim students' organisations and societies (Tyrer, 2004) rather than the effects on Muslim students themselves. Young Muslim women told us of several incidents of verbal abuse in public places after 9/11:

> It was after September 11th I was walking towards the bus stop to go to school and this man started shouting f*** Osama bin Laden is this and the other and started pointing to us saying Osama bin Laden as if where terrorists. That was very uncomfortable. (Khaleda Yousaf, Bangladeshi sixth-former, Leeds)

> We were in town just after September 11th attack. It was me and my sisters and we all wear scarves and we were walking past this guy who said something like, 'Pakis everywhere'. (Saira Begum, Bangladeshi sixth-former, Leeds)

> My dad's mosque was firebombed after September the 11th. We had petrol bombs put through the letter box. (Samreen Patel, Pakistani graduate, Leeds)

After the September 11 attacks many had to face questions at school or university about their religion and what it really meant. This demonstrates in a very vivid way how educational institutions are not insulated from wider events that may provoke racist or Islamophobic incidents. The events of 2001 have thus added further public pressure on individual Muslim students to justify and defend their faith and identity when interacting with non-Muslims in educational institutions. Shahida Azam, an Indian Muslim undergraduate in Leeds, described the situation in the following way:

> There's always that kind of tension of always being put on the spot and always being made to feel like you have to clarify your position that you disagree with the terrorists and all that kind of thing. I mean you're made to feel like an outsider in terms of you're always being told to condemn terrorism even though you shouldn't have to obviously it goes against what you believe I think particularly my Muslim identity that's where I feel it's always being questioned.

The young women responded to these experiences largely by ignoring them. Parents advised their daughters to do this; according to Sabreena Choudhary: 'they have sat down and told me that if anyone is ever racist towards you, just ignore them because if you retaliate it will only get worse.' However, some have reconsidered how they dress in response to specifically anti-Muslim comments and behaviour, to the extent of considering no longer wearing the *hijab*:

> You get comments, especially wearing *hijab*. Once me and my friends were in Manchester and there was a group of rugby fans, there was a match on, we walked past and they said 'they're everywhere them lot' as if they couldn't get away from us, there was so many Asians, Pakistanis and Muslims that you can't really miss them. If we think if we're in a situation like that again, where you feel quite vulnerable or in an enclosed space, we would probably take off *hijab*, if we felt in danger, that would be the most sensible thing ... I wouldn't do it in front of them, and I wouldn't let them think they'd won, but if I came into a situation that may lead to them doing something, I would discreetly remove it if I felt in danger. (Hikmat Bibi, Pakistani undergraduate, Leeds)

This again illustrates the emotional impact of the experience of explicit racism. In this instance, it is experienced as an assault on the self-identity of the women affected. Hikmat was so affected by this that she considered removing her *hijab*, the physical expression of her ethnic and religious identity as a woman.

Memories of racism at school

In relation to their experiences at school, the young women talked about the stereotyped views that some teachers apparently had of them. As other researchers have found, first experiences of racism are often at school from staff and other children (Bird, 1996; Clarke, 2000; Connolly, 1998). The assumptions in some cases were seen as being buttressed by public comments made by prominent local politicians. This illustrates the ways in which schools and universities are not insulated from the outside world, and why it is important to locate the racisms of the school and the university in relation to wider political events and discourses. According to Tahira Safder, a Pakistani graduate in Leeds:

> I have heard of cases where a lot of teachers still think that a lot of Asian women are not being allowed onto further studies and that as soon as they turn sixteen they are shipped off to Pakistan to get married. Most of this stuff is fomented by our local MP Ann Cryer she made many comments on how women should not be getting married until they have gone on to university and things and these comments are aimed at the Pakistanis and Bangladeshis.

The women were very critical of some staff in schools who had showed a lack of interest in South Asian pupils. Many of the women that we interviewed had either encountered or heard about teachers who did not take the education of young South Asian women seriously. This seemed to apply especially to Bangladeshi, Pakistani and working-class Indian, often Sikh, students. They told us that this minority of teachers often quite openly commented that South Asian women's education was going to be a waste of time as they were only destined for marriage and motherhood rather than for careers. This is a feature that others have uncovered in South Asian girls' experiences of school (Bird, 1996). As Bhatti concluded in her study of South Asian children at school:

> The majority view about Asian women prevalent at school was that they did not go out to work and that the girls too would therefore not go out to work; that they would get married quickly or that they would stay at home till they get married. The tenacity with which these stereotypical views persisted even after several discussions was surprising. (Bhatti, 1999: 220)

This implies rather demeaning assumptions about motherhood as well as South Asians, and we found evidence of the continued prevalence of such views from the experiences of the young women in our interviews. For instance, according to Jasvinder Kaur, a Sikh student:

> At school I just felt like some teachers didn't want to teach me because I was Asian, and I was stereotyped as an Asian. The teachers felt that we weren't interested in education and we didn't want to learn anything or we were a waste of time. I had one teacher who told me that I was fake basically, and just things like that – you see certain teachers, predominantly white, target Asian people.

Whilst at school and college, some women had voiced their dissatisfaction with the attitudes of some teachers, but in all the cases that we were told about this had been to no avail. Other researchers have encountered this failure of educational institutions to respond to students' complaints about racism (Bird, 1996; Bhatti, 1999). Parveen Ali, a Pakistani graduate, remembered her experience of racism from a college lecturer who refused to teach her and some other Asian women properly. Parveen and her friends reported him to the head of year in the college but he just did not want to get involved, as it may have left him short of teaching staff:

> He had this idea in his head that we as Asian women, our parents wouldn't allow us to go to uni, and he was just wasting his time teaching us. We spoke to the head of year and he just said 'Look, I'm stuck here, this man leaves college and I've got a whole class that I have no teacher for'. It was a really bad situation but the thing is, even though it was a really bad thing at the time, it was really distressing and really upsetting.

Some of the women felt that they suffered from racism within the education environment from fellow students, that was ignored by teaching staff. Naulta Begum recalled experiences of racism from the white girls towards her Bengali friends and herself at school. However, when they raised the matter with teachers, they found that the teachers were reluctant to intervene, leaving them to deal with the situation themselves:

> They didn't like the way we dressed and everything and they just started criticising every little thing we did so we told the teachers about it and they didn't do nothing about it ... (Naulta Begum, Bangladeshi sixth-former, Leeds)

Experiences of racism at university and beyond

At university, the racism experienced by young South Asian women also came from fellow students as well as staff. For the most part, this was often in the form of unacknowledged assumptions about what a young South Asian woman is like. These often revolved around what might be termed liberal stereotypes about oppressed South Asian women, especially Muslim women. For example, Zoreena Bibi, a Bangladeshi graduate in Leeds encountered such assumptions from fellow students. She felt that she was constantly having to correct white liberal myths about South Asian Muslim women that she felt were both racist and sexist in their failure to appreciate the change and diversity in South Asian communities:

> Talking to students they were like asking questions 'is your mum allowing you to come and study?' 'is your husband alright about it?', yeah there are myths ... you just have to tell them things are changing and put them right.

Assumptions about Muslims also crept into the teaching context in those subjects where issues around the relationship between Islam and the West were encountered. This raised issues about racism in the curriculum of universities (Bird, 1996). In one case, the Muslim students in the lecture felt uncomfortable about the way the topic was treated by the lecturer. As Zainab Ali, a Bangladeshi graduate in Leeds, recalled:

> ... one of my lecturers whilst giving a lecture on enlightenment and stuff it made me and a few of my other Muslim friends we kind of felt that we are being discriminated against, and that he didn't really like Muslims. That's one time when I felt a bit scared that a lecturer is trying to put his personal views across when he should have been objective.

Some others told us of explicitly negative comments or actions by a few members of the academic staff, who questioned their academic ability. Samreen Patel, a Pakistani graduate who had gone on to complete a PhD, told us of her experience in a department that had few British ethic minority students as undergraduates, but many international students at postgraduate level: 'When I was doing my MA I had a lecturer here in the xx department, who when I told him I was going to do a PhD laughed in my face ...'

Amongst the young women who had graduated, many were finding it difficult to obtain graduate level jobs, a phenomenon recently highlighted by the Equal Opportunities Commission (EOC, 2006). Whilst we did not specifically ask about racism in postgraduate employment in detail, some of the graduates told us about experiences of racism after graduation in response to our general questions about their experiences of racism. These often combined racist and sexist assumptions. Parveen Ali, for example, had problems getting a training contract after she had qualified as a solicitor. Even when she did obtain a place with a firm of South Asian male solicitors, it was not quite what she was expecting:

> I just found it really, really difficult, being an Asian female to find a training contract. I know it sounds like a silly thing to say, but people just look at you differently, because they think – 'God, what she's twenty-something now, she's obviously going to get married soon, then she's going to have kids, is it worth us investing the money that we're going to have to invest in getting her to qualify as a solicitor, the next thing you know, she'll be taking maternity leave, do we really want to go down that road?' Then I started working at a criminal law practice initially, in Leeds, for a group of Asian men, who had just set up a criminal law practice. I started working for them, and it wasn't quite what I expected it to be. I think they took advantage of the fact that I was Asian, that I was female and I was making far too many cups of tea, etc, so I left.

Those graduates who were considering academic careers were put off in a different way. The racism and sexism of academic life was referred to in ways that discouraged them from taking their careers further in higher education. For example, Samreen Patel, a Pakistani graduate in Leeds who had completed her PhD, was told by one of her white male academic mentors:

> You shouldn't go for a career in academia because you'll never be a professor because no Asian woman will ever become a professor in this country. You know at which point I thought that's it I have to, you know, how dare I not be a professor and now I have to. I'm not sure that I want to be now.

Whilst the academic who said this thought he was making a realistic assessment of the difficulties facing South Asian women due to discrimination, the effect of his comment was to reinforce that discrimination. As Clarke (2000: 520) argues, such comments might be well-meaning from the perspective of the academic, but the unintended consequence is racist.

Conclusions

Whilst much of the recent focus on racism in universities has been upon institutional racism imbued in their culture and routines (Law *et al*, 2004), we have documented evidence of South Asian women's experience of racism at the inter-personal level, inside and outside educational establishments. This acts as a further barrier to their educational and career success. Within universities, experiences of racism seemed more likely to occur in those institutions or departments that lacked a critical mass of South Asian women. Further research would be necessary to confirm this finding. Furthermore, the forms of racism experienced often combined assumptions about both gender and the culture of British South Asian communities. In addition, much of the racism experienced was really Islamophobia directed at both Muslim and non-Muslim students.

In terms of empirical evidence about the experience of racism, we have documented a number of important issues. To begin with, there is the rise of Islamophobia in Britain since 9/11. This demonstrates two aspects of everyday racism that are often overlooked in previous analyses. Firstly, racism and Islamophobia in particular are locked into global processes and events. This means that quite local instances of racial harassment and name-calling are enactments of responses to events that might seem quite remote. However, dominant representations of Muslims in the media and by mainstream politicians provide the themes and justifications for Islamophobic actions (Bagguley and Hussain, in press; Hussain and Bagguley, in press). Secondly, Muslim women are singled out for a particular gendered form of Islamophobia given that their style of dress, if they wear *hijab* for instance, marks them out as visibly Muslim. As university students, South Asian Muslim women are not insulated from this either outside or inside the institution.

Theoretically, we have tried to build upon previous work on racism in schools and youth clubs as well as universities, whilst combining this with new insights from feminist theories of critical mass. This has enabled us to understand more effectively the patterns of racism experienced by South Asian women in universities, and to examine the different ways in which they are able to resist and survive it. Whilst much of what we have found illustrates a continuity of the established forms of racism towards South Asian women in terms of their sexual and racial othering by white people, we have tried to understand the variations in this through using the idea of critical mass. Where the numbers of South Asian women reach a certain level in a university or a degree course, then their experiences of higher education become more positive. They are less likely to report racist experiences and there are sufficient numbers of them to form their own support networks within the institution. And they are less likely to feel like a fish out of water and to identify positively with a university that truly belongs to them.

8

Conclusion

The position of South Asian women in contemporary Britain is changing rapidly, and their increasing levels of attendance at university and the life chances this affords them are central to this change. Whilst this is partly explained by the expansion of the British university system from an élite to a mass form of higher education, we have seen that young South Asian women have disproportionately taken up these new opportunities. Young Indian women have been at the forefront of this move up to higher education, but they are now closely followed by Pakistani and Bangladeshi women as well. Throughout this book, we have been at pains to consider the differences between these three ethnic groups, who have often simply been lumped together as South Asian, black or ethnic minority. However, the significant differences between them in terms of their chances of getting to university, where and what they study, are also related in complex ways to religious expectations, class constraints and family expectations.

Most striking has been the growth in the numbers of Bangladeshi and Pakistani women going to university and obtaining degrees. In 1979, less than two per cent of the women from these backgrounds went to university, but the 2001 Census of Population revealed that 25 per cent of young Pakistani women and over fifteen per cent of young Bangladeshi women have degree level qualifications. For the women in these ethnic minority communities, this is a major shift in expectations and experiences between the generations, which is indicative of major cultural, social and economic transformations within them. These broad statistics as well as our interviews with young women from these communities told us the same story. It is now normal and expected that many if not most young women from these communities will go on to university with the active support and encouragement of their families. This is an image which clashes with the dominant political and media representations of South Asian Muslim women.

However, beneath this veneer of success is a more complex picture. Over this period of expansion of higher education for South Asian women, there has also been a shift in their subject preferences from what were seen as the typical South Asian subjects such as Medicine and Law to Business and Administration and other vocationally oriented subjects. This shift, as well as the overall growth in South Asian women graduates, is a reflection of the success of South Asian women's negotiations with their parents regarding their higher education. They are increasingly obtaining the support of their parents for their decision to go to university and for their own choice of subject.

There are a variety of reasons for this. Women are in stronger positions within these communities due to successful role models. Parents are rather less likely than was the case previously to see higher education as a source of potential threats to family *izzat*. For the Muslim women, their growth of understanding of Islamic thought has enabled them to show their parents that there are no religious restrictions on education for women. However, many of the Muslim women find that they have to compromise by choosing from a limited range of local universities within daily commuting distance in order to win the active support of their parents.

There remain significant inequalities in access to universities, where South Asian women tend to be concentrated in new universities with fewer resources and lower status. This may disadvantage them in their later careers. The level of A level qualifications and the preference of some institutions for A levels as opposed to vocational qualifications disadvantage many South Asian women. Whilst class divisions remain an important factor affecting whether or not white students get to university, this does not seem to be the case for South Asian women, for whom ethnicity remains important. Furthermore, whilst having a degree significantly improves South Asian women's chances of not being unemployed or obtaining better paid employment, as graduates they are still disadvantaged in the labour market in comparison to white women.

Through our analysis of our interviews with South Asian women, we have argued that their gendered ethnic and religious identities, and how they are changing, is central to understanding these changes and the continuing disadvantages. This generation of women think of themselves as British citizens with varying degrees of identification with their parents' cultures and homelands. For the Muslim women in particular, their religious identity is paramount in the light of wider political events. In order to sustain these identities, they do not engage in intergenerational conflict with their parents, but rather seek to negotiate the differences. Whilst for some this may mean that their choice of university is geographically limited, they are often acutely aware of the different statuses of the local universities. Apart from Oxford and Cambridge, which the most able reject for their class elitism and perceived whiteness, their choices are not driven by the ethnic composition of the student bodies.

We have found that the young women pursued a range of different financial strategies to fund their way through higher education. Whether they used a mixed economy of support, relied almost entirely upon parents or drew extensively on loans, they always acted strategically in a complex, morally regulated financial environment. Student finance has a been a major national policy question in education over the past fifteen years, and the system used by the women in this study has now been replaced, yet these policy debates have often ignored two important matters. Firstly, they have not given sufficient attention to the needs of various minority groups such as South Asian women. Secondly, they have ignored the ways in which students operate with respect to finance, taking account of the expectations of others in their decisions. Central to this strategic thinking is the moral economy of beliefs including religious beliefs which constrain choices, and rule out some opportunities, but also enable other kinds of family-based financial support.

When going to university, many young South Asian women are entering an environment that is more radically different for them than for the majority of their white, middle-class peers. Most of the people alongside them at their lectures have never seen a Bollywood movie, cannot speak a word of Punjabi and think India is a nice place to spend a gap year. That may be a stereotype of white middle-class undergraduates but, as we have seen, some of those students and indeed staff in universities make stereotypical assumptions about South Asian women.

What most significantly affected young women's experiences of isolation, racism and Islamophobia at university was whether or not there was a critical mass of other South Asian women on their course or at their university. Such a critical mass enabled the young women to create viable support groups with others who understood them and their problems in life. Questions of racism and Islamophobia in universities have all too often been brushed aside as a problem of the outside world, or as something that does not happen in higher institutions of learning due to their academic detachment. However, global events such as 9/11 have affected South Asian Muslim women in universities.

We would not like to end with a negative conclusion, and want to emphasise the broad picture of success. This success has partly been brought about by the growth of mass higher education, but more important have been ongoing changes between the generations and between men and women within the South Asian diaspora in Britain. Central to these changes has been the ability of young South Asian women of all ethnic origins, religious and class backgrounds to transform themselves and their communities.

References

Abbas, T (2004) *The Education of British South Asians*. London: Palgrave

Abbas, T (2005) *Muslim Britain: Communities under Pressure*. London: Zed Books

Afshar, H (1989a) Gender Roles and the Moral Economy of Kin among Pakistani Women in West Yorkshire *New Community* 15(2) 211-15

Afshar, H (1989b) Education: Hopes, expectations and achievements of Muslim women in West Yorkshire *Gender and Education* 1(3) 261-72

Afshar, H (1994) Muslim Women In West Yorkshire: Growing Up With Real and Imaginary Values Amidst Conflicting Views Of Self And Society in H Afshar and M Maynard (eds) *The Dynamics Of Race And Gender*. London: Taylor and Francis

Ahmad, F (2001) Modern Traditions? British Muslim Women and Academic Achievement *Gender and Education* 13: 137-52

Ahmed, F *et al* (2003) *South Asian women and Employment in Britain: the interaction of gender and ethnicity* London: PSI

Ahmad, F (2003) Still in Progress? Methodological Dilemmas, Tensions and Contradictions in Theorizing South Asian Muslim Women in N Puwar and P Raghuram (eds) *South Asian Women in the Diaspora*. Oxford: Berg

Anwar, M (1998) *Between Cultures*. London: Routledge

Archer, L and Hutchings, M (2000) Bettering Yourself? Discourses of Risk, Cost and Benefit in Ethnically Diverse, Young Working-class Non-participants' Constructions of Higher Education *British Journal of Sociology of Education* 21(4) 555-74

Archer, L *et al* (2003) *Higher Education and Social Class: Issues of Exclusion and Inclusion*. London: RoutledgeFalmer

Back, L (1996) *New Ethnicities and Urban Culture: Racisms and Multiculture in Young Lives*. London: Routledge

Bagguley, P and Hussain, Y (2005) Flying the Flag for England? Citizenship, Religion and Cultural Identity among British Pakistani Muslims in T Abbas (ed) *Muslim Britain: Communities under Pressure*. London: Zed Press

Bagguley, P and Hussain, Y (2006) Conflict and Cohesion: Official Constructions of 'Community' Around the 2001 'Riots' in Britain in S Herbrechter and M Higgins (eds) *Returning (to) Communities: Theory, culture and political practice of the communal*. Amsterdam: Rodopi

Bagguley, P and Hussain, Y (2007) *The Role of Higher Education in Providing Opportunities for South Asian Women*. Bristol: The Policy Press

Bagguley, P and Hussain, Y (forthcoming) Non-Muslim Responses to the 7th July Bombings in London in D Zimmerman (ed) *Terrorism and Diaspora*. Zurich: Centre for Security Studies.

145

Ball, S J (2003) *Class Strategies and the Educational Market: the Middle Classes and Social Advantage*. London: RoutledgeFalmer

Ball, S J *et al* (2002) Ethnic Choosing: Minority Ethnic Students, Social Class and Higher Education Choice *Race, Ethnicity and Education* 5(4) 333-57

Ballard, R and Vellins, S (1985) South Asian Entrants to British Universities: a Comparative Note *New Community* 12(2) 260-5

Ballard, R (1994) Introduction: The Emergence of Des Pardesh in R Ballard (ed) *Des Pardesh: The South Asian Presence in Britain*. London: Hurst and Company

Barone, C (2006) Cultural Capital, Ambition and the Explanation of Inequalities in Learning Outcomes: A Comparative Analysis. *Sociology* 40(6) 1039-58

Bhachu, P (1991a) Ethnicity Constructed and Reconstructed: the Role of Sikh Women in Cultural Elaboration and Educational Decision-making in Britain. *Gender and Education* 3(1) 45-60

Bhachu, P (1991b) Culture, Ethnicity and Class Among Punjabi Sikh Women in 1990s Britain *New Community* 17(3) 401-12

Bhatti, G (1999) *Asian Children at Home and at School: an Ethnographic Study*. London: Routledge

Bhopal, K (1997a) *Gender, Race and Patriarchy*. Aldershot: Ashgate

Bhopal, K (1997b) South Asian Women within Households: Dowries, Degradation And Despair *Women's Studies International Forum* 27(4)

Bhopal, K (1998) How Gender and Ethnicity Intersect: The Significance of Education, Employment and Marital Status. *Sociological Research Online* 3(3) http://wwwsocresonlineorguk/socresonline/3/3/6html

Bhopal, K (1999) South Asian Women and Arranged Marriages in East London in R Barot *et al* (eds) *Ethnicity, Gender and Social Change*. London: Palgrave

Bhopal, K (2000) South Asian Women in East London: The Impact of Education *European Journal of Women's Studies* 7(1)

Bird, J (1996) *Black Students and Higher Education: Rhetorics and Realities*. Buckingham: Open University Press

Blackburn, R M and Jarman, J (1993) Changing Inequalities in Access to British Universities *Oxford Review of Education* 19(2) 197-215

Bourdieu, P (1997) The Forms of Capital in A H Halsey *et al* (eds) *Education: Culture, Economy, Society*. Oxford: Oxford University Press

Brah, A (1993) *Cartographies of Diaspora: Contesting Identities*. London: Routledge

Brah, A and Minhas, R (1985) Structural Racism or Cultural Difference, in G Weiner (ed) *Just a Bunch of Girls*. Milton Keynes: Open University Press

Brooks, R (2004) My Mum Would be as Pleased as Punch if I Actually Went, but my Dad seems a bit more particular about it: Parental Involvement in Young People's Higher Education Choices *British Educational Research Journal* 30(4) 495-514

Callender, C (2001) Changing Student Finances in Higher Education: Policy Contradictions under New Labour *Widening Participation and Lifelong Learning*, 3(2) 5-15

Callender, C (2003) Student Financial Support in Higher Education: Access and Exclusion in M Tight (ed) *Access and Exclusion*. London: JAI Press

Callender, C and Jackson, J (2004) *Fear of Debt and Higher Education Participation*. London: South Bank University

Callender, C and Kemp, M (2000) *Changing Student Finances: Income, Expenditure and the Take up of Loans among Full- and Part-time Higher Education Students in 1998/9*. London: DfEE

Cantle, T (2001) *Community Cohesion: A Report of the Independent Review Team* London: Home Office

Carter, J *et al* (1999) *Ethnicity and Employment in Higher Education.* London: PSI

Cheng, Y and Heath, A (1993) Ethnic Origins and Class Destinations *Oxford Review of Education* 19(20) 151-65

Clark, K and Drinkwater, D (2005) Some Preliminary Findings on Ethnic Minority Labour Market Activity using Controlled Access *Microdata SARS Newsletter* February, Manchester: University of Manchester

Clarke S (2000) Experiencing Racism in Higher Education *Socio-Analysis* 2(1) 47-63

Coleman, J S (1997) Social Capital in the Creation of Human Capital in A H Halsey *et al* (eds) *Education: Culture, Economy, Society.* Oxford: Oxford University Press

Connolly, P (1998) *Racism, Gender Identities and Young Children.* London: Routledge

Connor, H (2001) Deciding For or Against Participation in Higher Education: the Views of Young People from Lower Social Class Backgrounds *Higher Education Quarterly* 55 (2) 204-24

Connor, H *et al* (2001) *The Right Choice?* London: Universities UK

Connor, H *et al* (2004) *Why the Difference? A Closer Look at Higher Education Minority Ethnic Students and Graduates.* DfES Research Report RR552

Connor, H *et al* (2006) *Progressing to Higher Education: Vocational Qualifications and Admissions.* Ormskirk: Action on Access

Crow, G (1989) The Use of the Concept of Strategy in Recent Sociological Literature *Sociology* 23(1) 1-24

Crown Prosecution Service (2005) *Racist Incident Monitoring: Annual Report 2004/2005.* London: Crown Prosecution Service

Crozier, G and Davies, J (2006) Family Matters: a Discussion of the Bangladeshi and Pakistani Extended Family and Community in Supporting the Children's Education *The Sociological Review* 54(4) 678-95

Dahlerup, D (1988) From a Small to a Large Minority: Women in Scandinavian Politics *Scandinavian Political Studies* 11(2) 275-98

Dale, A *et al* (2002) Routes into Education and Employment for Young Pakistani and Bangladeshi Women in the UK *Ethnic and Racial Studies* 25(6) 942-68

Dale, A *et al* (2002) The Labour Market Prospects for Pakistani and Bangladeshi Women *Work Employment and Society* 16(1) 5-25

Dale A *et al* (2006) A Life-course Perspective on Ethnic Differences in Women's Economic Activity in Britain *European Sociological Review* 22 323-37

Dearing, R (1997) *Higher Education in the Learning Society: the Report of the National Committee of Inquiry into Higher Education* (the Dearing Report). London: The Stationery Office

Demack, S *et al* (2000) Minding the Gap: Ethnic, Gender and Social Class Differences in Attainment at 16, 1988-95 *Race, Ethnicity and Education* 3(2) 117-43

Denham, J (2002) *Building Cohesive Communities: A Report of the Ministerial Group on Public Order and Community Cohesion.* London: Home Office

Department for Communities and Local Government (2006) *2005 Citizenship Survey: Race and Faith Topic Report.* London: Department for Communities and Local Government

Department of Work and Pensions (2006) *Households below Average Income 2004-05.* London: the stationery office

Devine, F (2004) *Class Practices: how Parents Help their Children get Good Jobs.* Cambridge: Cambridge University Press

Din, I (2006) *The New British: the Impact of Culture and Community on Young Pakistanis*. Aldershot: Ashgate

Drury, B (1991) Sikh Girls and the Maintenance of an Ethnic Culture *New Community* 17(3) 387-99

Drury, B (1996) The Impact of Religion, Culture, Racism and Politics on the Multiple Identities of Sikh Girls in T Ranger *et al* (eds) *Culture, Identity and Politics*. Aldershot: Ashgate

Dwyer, C *et al* (2006) Ethnicity as Social Capital? Explaining the Differential Achievements of Young British Pakistani Men and Women, paper presented at the Ethnicity, Mobility and Society Conference, University of Bristol

Dwyer, C (1999a) Contradictions of Community: Questions of Identity for Young British Muslim Women *Environment and Planning* A 31: 53-68

Dwyer, C (1999b) Veiled Meanings: Young British Muslim Women and the Negotiation of Differences *Gender, Place and Culture* 6(1) 5-26

Egerton, M and Halsey, A H (1993) Trends by Social Class and Gender in Access to Higher Education in *Britain Oxford Review of Education* 19(2) 183-96

Elster, J (1979) *Ulysses and the Sirens: Studies in Rationality and Irrationality*. Cambridge: Cambridge University Press

EOC, (2006) *Moving on up? Bangladeshi, Pakistani and Black Caribbean women and work*. Manchester: Equal Opportunities Commission

Feagin, J R *et al* (1996) *The Agony of Education: Black Students at White Colleges and Universities*. London: Routledge

Finch, S *et al* (2006) Student Income and Expenditure Survey: 2004/05, *Research Report RR725*. Nottingham: Department for Education and Skills

Forsyth, A and Furlong, A (2000) *Socioeconomic Disadvantage and Access to Higher Education*. Bristol: the Policy Press

Foster, KM (2005) Diet of Disparagement: the Racial Experiences of Black Students in a Predominately White University, *International Journal of Qualitative Studies in Education* 18(4) 489-505

Gardner, K and Shukur, A (1994) 'I'm Bengali, I'm Asian and I'm Living Here': The Changing Identity Of British Bengalis in R Ballard (ed) *Des Pardesh: The South Asian Presence in Britain*. London: Hurst and Company

Ghuman, P (1994) *Coping With Two Cultures*. Bristol: Longdum

The Guardian, 6 October 2006 Take off the Veil says Straw – to the Immediate Anger from Muslims

The Guardian, 25 November 2006 School Assistant who would not Compromise over Veil is Sacked

The Guardian, 20 December 2006 Beshenivesky Suspect fled Britain Wearing Veil

Hall, S (1990) Cultural Identity and Diaspora in J Rutherford (ed) *Identity: Community, Culture, Difference*. London: Lawrence and Wishart

Halsey, A H *et al* (1980) *Origins and Destinations: Family, Class, and Education in Modern Britain*. Oxford: Clarendon Press

Haque, Z (2000) The Ethnic Minority Underachieving Group? Investigating the Claims of Underachievement amongst Bangladeshi Pupils in British Secondary Schools *Race, Ethnicity and Education* 3(2) 145-68

Heath, A and McMahon, D (1997) Education and Occupational Attainments: the Impact of Ethnic Origins in V Karn (ed) *Ethnicity in the 1991 census Vol 4, Employment, Education and Housing among the Ethnic Minority Populations of Great Britain*. London: The Stationery Office

Housee, S (2004) Unveiling South Asian Female Identities post September 11; Asian Female Students' Sense of Identity and Experiences of Higher Education in I Law *et al* (eds) (2004) *Institutional Racism in Higher Education*. Stoke-on-Trent: Trentham Books

Hussain, Y (2005) *Writing Diaspora: South Asian Women, Culture and Ethnicity.* Aldershot: Ashgate

Hussain, Y and Bagguley, P (2005) Citizenship as Identity: British Pakistanis After the 2001 Riots *Sociology* 39(3) 407-25

Hussain, Y and Bagguley, P (forthcoming) Muslim Responses to the 7th July Bombings in London in D Zimmerman (ed) *Terrorism and Diaspora*. Zurich: Centre for Security Studies

Jacobson, J (1997) Religion and Ethnicity: Dual and Alternative Sources of Identity among Young British Pakistanis *Ethnic and Racial Studies* 20(2) 238-56

Jenkins, R (1997) *Rethinking Ethnicity: Arguments and Explorations.* Sage: London

Jones, T (1993) *Britain's Ethnic Minorities.* London: PSI

Joly, D (1995) *Britannia's Crescent: Making a Place for Muslims in British Society.* Aldershot: Ashgate

Kalra, S S (1980) *Daughters of Tradition: Adolescent Sikh Girls and their Accommodation to Life in British Society*. London: Third World Publications

Kalra, V S *et al* (2005) *Diaspora and Hybridity.* London: Sage

Kanter, R M (1977) *Men and Women of the Corporation.* New York: Basic Books

Khanum, S (1995) Education and the Muslim Girl, in M Blair *et al* (eds) *Identity and Diversity; Gender and the Experience of Education.* Clevedon: Multilingual Matters

Khattab, N (2005) *Inequalities and Polarities in Educational Achievement amongst Britain's Ethnic Minorities*. Department of Sociology, University of Bristol, Bristol

Law, I *et al* (eds) (2004) *Institutional Racism in Higher Education.* Stoke-on-Trent: Trentham Books

Leslie, D and Drinkwater, S (1999) Staying on in Full-time Education: Reasons for Higher Participation Rates among Ethnic Minority Males and Females *Economica* 66: 63-77

Lindley, J *et al* (2006) Ethnic Differences in Women's Employment: the Changing Role of Qualifications *Oxford Economic Papers* 58: 351-78

Lovenduski, J (2001) Women and Politics: Minority Representation or Critical Mass? *Parliamentary Affairs* 51: 743-58

Low Pay Commission (2005) *National Minimum Wage: Low Pay Commission Report Cmd 6475.* London: The Stationery Office

McManus, I C *et al* (1995) Medical School Applicants from Ethnic Minority Groups: Identifying if and when they are Disadvantaged *British Medical Journal* 310: 496-500

McManus, I C *et al* (1998) Factors affecting Likelihood of Applicants being Offered a Place in Medical Schools in the United Kingdom in 1996 and 1997: a Retrospective Study *British Medical Journal* 317: 1111-7

Merton, R K (1963) *Social Theory and Social Structure.* Glencoe Illinois: Social Press

Modood, T (1993) The Number of Ethnic Minority Students in British Higher Education: some Grounds for Optimism *Oxford Review of Education* 19(2) 167-82

Modood, T (1994) Political Blackness and British Asians *Sociology* 28(4) 859-76

Modood, T *et al* (1997) *Diversity and Disadvantage* (The Fourth PSI Survey). London: PSI

Modood, T (2004) Capitals, Ethnic Identity and Educational Qualifications *Cultural Trends* 13(2) 87-105

Modood, T (2005) The Educational Attainments of Ethnic Minorities in Britain in G C Loury *et al* (eds) *Ethnicity, Social Mobility and Public Policy: Comparing the US and the UK.* Cambridge: Cambridge University Press

Modood, T and Shiner, M (1994) *Ethnic Minorities and Higher Education – Why are there Different Rates of Entry?* London: PSI

Morgan, Y J *et al* (1999) Decision-Making Behaviour of Potential Higher Education Students *Higher Education Quarterly*, 53(3) 211-28

Mouzelis, N (1995) *Sociological Theory: What Went Wrong? Diagnosis and Remedies.* London: Routledge

Nash, R (1999) Realism in the Sociology of Education: 'Explaining' Social Differences in Attainment *British Journal of Sociology of Education* 20(1) 107-25

National Audit Office (2002) *Widening Participation in Higher Education in England: Report by the Comptroller and Auditor General, HC 485, Session 2001-2.* London: The Stationery Office

Neville-Jones, P (2007) *Uniting the Country: Interim Report of the National and International Security Policy Group on National Cohesion.* London: The Conservative Party

Owen, C *et al* (1997) Higher Education Qualifications, in V Karn (ed) *Ethnicity in the 1991 census Vol 4, Employment, Education and Housing among the Ethnic Minority Populations of Great Britain.* London: The Stationery Office

Papastergiadis, N (1997) Tracing Hybridity in Theory in P Werbner and Modood, T (eds) *Debating Cultural Hybridity; Multi-Cultural Identities and the Politics of Anti-Racism.* London: Zed Books

Parmar, P (1982) Gender, Race and Class: Asian Women in Resistance, in *Centre for Contemporary Cultural Studies The Empire Strikes Back: Race and Racism in 70s Britain.* London: Hutchinson

Payne, J and Callender, C (1997) *Student Loans: Who Borrows and Why?* London: Policy Studies Institute

Peach, C (2006) Muslims in the 2001 Census of England and Wales: Gender and Economic Disadvantage *Ethnic and Racial Studies* 29: 629-55

Penn, R and Scattergood, H (1992) Ethnicity and Career Aspirations in Contemporary Britain *New Community* 19(1) 75-98

Pennell, H and West, A (2005) The Impact of Increased Fees on Participation in Higher Education in England *Higher Education Quarterly* 59(2) 127-37

Phoenix, A (2005) Remembered Racialisation: Young People and Positioning in Differential Understandings in K Murji and J Solomos (eds) *Racialisation: Studies in Theory and Practice.* Oxford: Oxford University Press

Platt, L (2002) *Parallel Lives? Poverty among Ethnic Minority Groups in Britain.* London: Child Poverty Action Group

Pugsley, L (1998) Throwing Your Brains at it: Higher Education, Markets and Choice International Studies in *Sociology of Education* 8(1) 71-92

Puwar, N (2004) Fish in and out of water: a Theoretical Framework for Race and the Space of Academia, in Law, I *et al* (eds) (2004) *Institutional Racism in Higher Education.* Stoke-on-Trent: Trentham Books

Ranger , T *et al* (eds) (1996) *Culture, Identity and Politics.* Aldershot: Ashgate

Rassool, N (1999) Flexible Identities: Exploring Race and Gender Issues among a Group of Immigrant Pupils in an Inner-city Comprehensive School *British Journal of Sociology of Education* 20(1) 23-36

Read, B *et al* (2003) Challenging Cultures? Student Conceptions of Belonging and Isolation at a Post-1992 University *Studies in Higher Education* 28(3) 261-77

Reay, D *et al* (2005) *Degrees of Choice: Social Class, Race and Gender in Higher Education.* Stoke: Trentham Books

Rutherford, J (ed) (1990) *Identity: Community, Culture, Difference.* London: Lawrence and Wishart

Samad, Y (1996) The Politics of Islamic Identity among Bangladeshis and Pakistanis in Britain in T Ranger *et al* (eds) *Culture, Identity and Politics.* Aldershot: Ashgate

Sayer, A (2004) *Approaching Moral Economy Cultural Economy Working Paper No. 6.* University of Lancaster: Lancaster

Seth, S (1985) Education of Asian Women in M Hughes and M Kennedy (eds) *New Futures: Changing Women's Education.* London: Routledge and Kegan Paul

Shain, F (2003) *The Schooling and Identity of Asian Girls.* Stoke-on-Trent: Trentham Books

Shaw, A (1994) The Pakistani Community in Oxford, in R Ballard (ed) *Desh Pardesh: The South Asian Presence in Britain.* London: Hurst and Company

Shaw, A (2000) *Kinship and Continuity: Pakistani Families in Britain.* Amsterdam: Harwood Academic Publishers

Shiner, M and Modood, T (2002) Help or Hindrance? Higher Education and the Route to Ethnic Inequality *British Journal of Sociology of Education* 23(2) 209-32

Singh, R (1990) Ethnic Minority Experience in Higher Education *Higher Education Quarterly* 44(4) 344-59

Stopes-Roe, M and Cochrane, R (1990) *Citizens of this Country: the Asian British.* Clevedon: Multilingual Matters

Tanna, K (1990) Excellence, Equality And Educational Reform: The Myth of South Asian Achievement Levels *New Community* 16(3) 349-68

Taylor, P (1993a) Ethnic Group Data and Applications to Higher Education *Higher Education Quarterly* 46(4) 359-74

Taylor, P (1993b) Minority Ethnic Groups and Gender in Access to Higher Education *New Community* 19(3) 425-40

Thornley, EP and Siann, G (1991) The Career Aspirations of South Asian Girls *Gender and Education* 3(3) 237-48

Tomlinson, S (1983) The Educational Performance of Children of Asian Origin *New Community* 10(3) 381-92

Troyna, B (1984) Fact or Artefact? The Educational Underachievement of Black Pupils *British Journal of the Sociology of Education* 17 361-75

Troyna, B (1987) *Racial Inequality in Education.* London: Tavistock

Troyna, B and Hatcher, R (1992) *Racism in Children's Lives: a Study of Mainly White Primary Schools.* London: Routledge

Tyrer, D (2004) The Others: Extremism and Intolerance on Campus and the Spectre of Islamic Fundamentalism in I Law *et al* (eds) (2004) *Institutional Racism in Higher Education.* Stoke-on-Trent: Trentham Books

Vellins, S (1982) South Asian Students in British Universities: a Statistical Note *New Community* 10(2) 206-12

Vertovec, S (1996) 'Diaspora' in E Cashmore (ed) *Dictionary of Race and Ethnic Relations* (4th Ed.). London: Routledge

Wade, B and Souter, P (1992) *Continuing To Think: The British Asian Girl.* London: Clevedon

Weale, M (1993) The Benefits of Higher Education: a Comparison of Universities and Polytechnics *Oxford Review of Economic Policy* 8(2) 35-47

Werbner, P (2005) Honour, Shame and the Politics of Sexual Embodiment among South Asian Muslims in Britain and Beyond: an Analysis of Debates in the Public Sphere *International Social Science Review* 6(1) 25-47

West, J and Pilgrim, S (1995) South Asian Women in Employment: the Impact of Migration, Ethnic origin and the Local Economy *New Community* 21(3) 357-78

Westwood, S and Hoffman, D (1979) *Asian Women: Education and Social Change*. Leicester: University Of Leicester

Whitehead, J M *et al* (2006) University Choice: What Influences the Decisions of Academically Successful Post-16 Students? *Higher Education Quarterly* 60(1) 4-26

Wilson, A (1978) *Finding A Voice*. London: Virago

Woodrow, M *et al* (2002) *Social Class and Participation: Good Practice in Widening Participation in Higher Education*. London: Universities UK

Wright, C (1992) *Race Relations in the Primary School*. London: David Fulton

Yin, R K (1984) *Case Study Research: Design and Methods*. Beverly Hills: Sage

Subject Index

age groups 12, 21

A levels 6, 10, 16, 19-20, 28, 58, 63-5, 68-9, 71, 79, 82, 84, 89, 142

Bangaldeshi women 1-2, 4, 5-7, 9-10, 16, 17, 20-24, 32-4, 38, 40-41, 45, 50, 54-5, 61-3, 65, 72-4, 80, 84, 88, 89-90, 92, 95, 97-8, 101-7, 123, 132, 135, 141-2

Birmingham 6, 23-4, 96, 106

Britishness 6, 37, 40, 46-9, 55

brothers, *see* siblings

Cambridge, University of 82-3, 85

Census of Population 2, 12, 21, 22, 23, 24, 141

clothing 6, 38, 40, 42-4, 48-55, 130, 134, 138

critical mass 7, 36, 125-6, 128, 129, 138-9, 143

cultural capital 3, 5, 28, 33-5, 84

Dearing Report 109

diaspora 2, 37-8, 54

ethnic groups, *see* ethnicity

ethnic identity, *see* ethnicity

ethnic inequalities 1, 9, 20, 27, 33

ethnic penalty 14, 18, 22

ethnic mix of universities 81-84, 125-30

ethnicity 2-3, 5-7, 17-19, 22-5, 27-9, 33-6, 37-55, 57-9, 64-5, 72-6, 78, 80, 87, 95, 110-1, 121-30, 141-4

family 2, 5, 25, 27, 28, 30, 31-3, 35, 42, 43, 52, 54-5, 58, 61, 63-4, 67, 71, 74, 80, 88, 94-5, 98, 106-7, 110-11, 113-14, 117-18, 141-3

financing degrees 4, 7, 27, 100, 109-19, 143

GCSE 16, 19-20

gender 2, 5, 8, 9, 10-14, 20, 25, 28, 29-31, 33-4, 37, 39, 57, 66, 127, 138

graduates 4, 13, 16, 22, 24, 25, 55, 59, 80, 102-4, 109-11, 113, 114-18, 122, 137, 142

hijab 7, 50-4, 55, 130-1, 133-4, 138

hindu 87-8, 91, 96-8, 100, 118

hybridity 2, 37, 38, 54, 55

identity 2-3, 5-6, 25-6, 35, 37-40, 47, 50-2, 54-5, 97, 107, 129, 133-4, 143

Indian women 2, 4, 5, 10-24, 28, 38, 40, 42-3, 51, 54-5, 60-2, 64-5, 67-8, 71-2, 74, 84, 88, 90-3, 96-8, 100-2, 105, 107, 128, 132, 135, 141

Islam 3, 5, 28, 31, 38-9, 44-5, 55, 110, 113, 136

Islamophobia 3, 7, 51, 55, 82, 124-5, 130-1, 133-4, 138, 143

izzat 32, 106-7, 142

labour market 1, 5, 21-3, 30, 62, 65, 68,102, 142

leaving home 6, 87-8, 96-8, 100-1, 105-6

Leeds 23, 24, 78-9, 96, 126

living at home 6, 79, 96-8, 100, 103, 114

marriage 6, 21, 30-2, 87-96, 102, 107, 128, 135

methodology 23-6

moral economy 3, 36, 111-12, 118, 143

Muslims 1, 4, 6, 38-9, 41-55, 59, 67, 71-4, 82, 87-8, 91, 94, 96, 98-104, 114-15, 123, 126, 130-1, 133-4, 136, 142-4

niqab 49, 51

Oxford, University of 79, 82-3, 85, 143

Pakistani women 2, 4, 5-7, 10-24, 30, 32-4, 38, 40, 43-4, 48, 50-5, 60-2, 64-5, 70-4, 80, 84, 89, 93-6, 98, 100-3, 106, 110, 122-3, 141-2

parents 2, 3, 6, 9, 10, 14,
    17-18, 25, 29-32, 34, 38,
    41-3, 45, 48, 50-5, 57-
    75, 79, 81, 84, 87-107,
    110-11, 113-16, 118, 142
pioneers 62-3

racial discrimination 10, 28,

racism 2-3, 5, 7, 31, 121-4,
    143-4
    – in universities 28-9, 36,
    124-5, 136-8
    – perceptions of 123
    – experiences of 55,
    122-3, 130-2, 134-8

sampling 24-5
SARS 12
school 14, 16, 19-20, 29, 30,
    55, 65, 71, 122-4, 134-6
siblings 2, 6, 25, 62, 74, 94,
    89, 98, 110, 114-15, 117-
    18
Sikhs 32, 38, 87, 88, 92, 96-
    8, 100, 118, 123, 128,
    135
sisters, see siblings
sixth formers 24, 66, 75, 88,
    104-7, 110, 112-13
social capital 3, 5, 26, 28,
    33-5, 58, 84

social class 4, 5, 6, 17-18,
    20, 22-3, 25, 27, 32, 33,
    35, 57-9, 61-2, 64, 66,
    71, 74, 79, 80, 85, 87,
    94, 96-8, 100, 102-3,
    105, 110, 119, 135, 143
strategy 3, 111-12, 114-18
student debt, see financing
    degrees
subjects
    – choice of 6, 16, 63-4,
    66-71, 84

UCAS 2, 15, 17, 18-19, 28,
    61, 64, 65
undergraduates 24, 58, 59,
    81, 98, 100, 107, 109,
    111, 114-18, 122, 137,
    143
unemployment 17, 21-2, 29
universities
    choice of 6, 7, 57, 79,
    81, 97, 98, 100, 107, 143
    decision to attend 24, 58,
    71-4
    perceptions of 74-9

veil, see hijab and niqab

West Midlands 23, 76-9, 81,
    96, 107, 126, 128
West Yorkshire 23, 76-9, 81,
    106, 107